Dynamics of Psychoanalytic Institutions

Dynamics of Psychoanalytic Institutions provides a thorough appraisal of the current state of psychoanalytic groups and how they might move forward under fraught conditions, representing the outcome of many years of work by the Institutional Matters Forum (IMF).

This erudite book presents the thoughts, experiences, reflections, and outcomes of the IMF, a long-standing working group of the European Psychoanalytical Federation (EPF). Organisational and group dynamic issues have a great influence on the life of psychoanalytic societies. However, they are often lived through as part of institutional and professional daily lives or retold as part of a history, marked with frequent conflicts, disruptions, splits, and impasses. This book recognises the need to explore the structure, culture, organisation, and unique characteristics of psychoanalytical organisations and to provide the space and tools for reflection. Consisting of seven psychoanalysts from seven different countries, the IMF group charts the origins of analytic societies, explores group mentality, and considers the impact on the global experience of war and the Covid pandemic on psychoanalytic institutions.

Jasminka Šuljagić is a training analyst and the former president of the Psycho-analytical Society of Serbia. She is a member and founder of the EPF Institutional Matters Forum, member and former general editor of the EPF Executive Board, and chair of the EPF Archive Committee. She has many presentations and publications in seven different languages.

"*Dynamics of Psychoanalytic Institutions: Legacy, Transformation and Becoming* is a much-needed and remarkable achievement for the understanding of one of the less-explored dimensions of our discipline which, at the same time, is a central one: our own institutions. Written by a group of the most well-known and experienced analysts in this field, this excellent book arrives at a moment when we all need to deepen our insights on how our institutions begun, developed, and must keep alive their vitality and the capacity to continue as a work in progress and continuous transformation."

Cláudio Laks Eizirik, *Former President of the International Psychoanalytic Association, and Professor Emeritus of Psychiatry, Federal University of Rio Grande do Sul, Brazil*

"Springing forth from the engagement with the individual psyche, its conflictual and needful nature, the contributions of psychoanalysis in the social realm have been marginalized. Lately, however, the exploration of institutional and societal issues has gradually grown to receive its fair share and equal status. This book, *Dynamics of Psychoanalytic Institutions, Legacy, Transformation and Becoming*, is a major step in this direction. The topics covered are fascinating and relevant to every major aspect of psychoanalytic institutional and organizational life. It offers a complex tapestry that keenly explores institutional developments, emphasizing their formative stages and historical circumstances, which both fertilize and restrict freedom and creativity. Far from idealizing, these dynamics are explored penetratingly through a psychoanalytic lens and with analytic neutrality. The issues considered are too numerous to list, ranging from the training of candidates to the splitting and rejoining of mature societies. It is equally striking that this important work on group and organizational dynamics is the product of a working group with different styles and backgrounds that succeeds in forming a rich and rewarding whole. It will undoubtedly be a major addition to this growing area of study and exploration."

Shmuel Erlich, *Professor (Emeritus), Sigmund Freud Chair, Hebrew University, and Past Chair, IPA Institutional Issues Committee*

Dynamics of Psychoanalytic Institutions

Legacy, Transformation and Becoming

Edited by Jasminka Šuljagić

R Routledge
Taylor & Francis Group

LONDON AND NEW YORK

Designed cover image: Shutterstock, Inc. | dastagir

First published 2025
by Routledge
4 Park Square, Milton Park, Abingdon, Oxon OX14 4RN

and by Routledge
605 Third Avenue, New York, NY 10158

Routledge is an imprint of the Taylor & Francis Group, an informa business

British Library Cataloguing-in-Publication Data
A catalogue record for this book is available from the British Library

ISBN: 978-1-032-70977-2 (hbk)
ISBN: 978-1-032-68622-6 (pbk)
ISBN: 978-1-032-70981-9 (ebk)

DOI: 10.4324/9781032709819

Typeset in Times New Roman
by Apex CoVantage, LLC

Contents

PART III
The Familiar and the Unfamiliar in
Psychoanalytic Institutions: About Stumbling
Across Otherness

PART IV
Paths and Figures of Intimacy Within
Psychoanalytic Rooms and Organisations

PART V
Institutional Life in Psychoanalytic Organisations

Contributors

Bernard Chervet is a psychiatrist and training psychoanalyst of the Psychoanalytical Society of Paris (SPP), the former president of the SPP, a representative on the IPA Board and on the IPA Executive Committee, and the Scientific Director of the Congress of French-Speaking Psychoanalysts (CPLF). He was the founder of *SPP Editions* and is the author of numerous publications in French, including international journals which cover a wide range of clinical and theoretical psychoanalytic topics. He was the winner of the Bouvet Prize in 2017 for all his work. He provided the keynote to the CPLF 2009 on the theme the après-coup and is the author of *Après-coup in Psychoanalysis: The Fulfilment of Desire and Thought* (Routledge). He is a contributor to the IPA encyclopaedic dictionary.

Christine Diercks is a psychiatrist and psychoanalyst, member, training analyst, and archivist of the Vienna Psychoanalytic Society. She was president of the Society 2005–2008 and 2013–2015 and initiated the Psychoanalytic Free Clinic (Ambulatorium) and the Vienna Psychoanalytic Academy. Her publications and research projects focus on psychoanalytic theory, clinic, and history of psychoanalytic institutions and biographies, 2006–2021, www.psyalpha.net, a digital platform for psychoanalysis (concept, contributions). Today she is editor of *psyalpha*, a digital platform for psychoanalysis; is a member of the forum Institutions Matter; and is the general editor of the *Sigmund Freud Edition*, the digital historical critical edition of Freud's entire writings and letters.

Franziska Ylander is a psychoanalyst and psychiatrist working in private practice and supervising analysts in training. She has a long-standing interest in institutional matters. She was actively engaged in the preparatory work for the fusion of two Swedish psychoanalytical societies, both component societies of IPA, into what has, since 2011, been the Swedish Psychoanalytic Association. She has held different positions within the Swedish Psychoanalytical Society and, later, the Swedish Psychoanalytical Association and particularly engaged herself in questions concerning clinical supervision and the development of training for supervisors. Between 2011 and 2016, she was the vice president of the European Psychoanalytic Federation (EPF) and the European representative at the Board of the IPA between 2017 and 2021. Since 2016, she has been a member of the EPF Forum of Institutional Matters.

Gábor Szőnyi (MD) is a training psychoanalyst (Hungarian Psychoanalytical Society) and a training group analyst (Institute of Group Analysis, Budapest) and also has a degree in sociology. During his professional career, he has held offices in the International Psychoanalytical Association, European Psychoanalytical Federation, International Association for Group Psychotherapy, and Group Analytic Society International. He was the editor-in-chief of the central Hungarian professional journal *Pszichoterápia*. He has been co-founder of the Outpatient Psychoanalytic Method Centre MentalPort/Budapest. Among others, he has participated in research on supervision, group process and outcome, utilisation of psychotherapy training, and psychoanalytic organisations. He is the author of two textbooks (in Hungarian – on the psychotherapies, respectively, on group leadership) and over 170 publications in psychoanalysis and in psychotherapy. His fields of interest are microprocess, supervision, and analytic organisations.

Jasminka Šuljagić is a training analyst of the Psychoanalytical Society of Serbia (since 2007), a former president (2012–2018) and currently works in private practice in Belgrade. She is a member and founder of the EPF Institutional Matters Forum (since 2015), an initiator of gatherings of neighbouring societies within a biannual conference, "Thinking on the Border" (since 2017), and a member of the ING Liaison Committee for the Bulgarian Society (since 2017). Jasminka is engaged in various activities within the European Psychoanalytic Federation, including organisation of the European Psychoanalytic Conference for University Students (EPCUS) (2016–2022). She is also a member of the EPF Executive Board as the general editor (2020–2024) and is the chair of the EPF Archive Committee (since 2023), with many presentations and publications.

Maggiorino Genta is a psychiatrist, training psychoanalyst (since 2007), and former president of the Swiss Psychoanalytical Society (2015–2018). He has been conducting theoretical and clinical seminars since 2000. He has given several speeches and participated in various panels, notably in Buenos Aires (2017) and Tokyo (2018). Since November 2015, he has been a member of the EPF ad hoc group on Institutional Matter (IMG), and he is now the chair of the Institutional Matters Forum (IMF). Since July 2017, he has been a member of an EPF group on "remote analysis".

Philip Stokoe is a psychoanalyst in private practice working with adults and couples and an organisational consultant with experience of a wide range of organisations. He has been a senior manager in a range of health and social care settings since 1978, finally working in the Adult Department of the Tavistock and Portman NHS Foundation Trust between 1994 and 2012, where he was appointed the clinical director in 2007. He has held several roles within the British Psychoanalytic Society and is a member of the European Psychoanalytic Federation Forum on Institutional Matters, which studies the nature of psycho-analytic institutions. He has written and taught on a wide range of subjects. His book *The Curiosity Drive: Our Need for Inquisitive Thinking* was published in 2020 and shortlisted for the Gradiva® Award for Best Book in 2021.

Acknowledgements

All the chapters in this book were originally written for EPF conferences and IPA congresses or presented as an invited talk. Part I, "On the Origin of Psychoanalytical Organisations", consists of papers delivered at the EPF conference, 2018, in Warsaw. Part II, "Infantile and Institutionalisation", belongs to the IPA congress held in Vancouver, 2021. The chapters from Part III, "The Familiar and the Unfamiliar in Psychoanalytic Institutions: About Stumbling Across Otherness", were presented at the EPF conference, 2017, in The Hague. Part IV, "Paths and Figures of Intimacy Within Psychoanalytic Rooms and Organisations", was written for the panel held at the IPA congress in Buenos Aires, 2017. Part V, "Institutional Life in Psychoanalytic Organisations", stems from different sources: of the open discussion at the IPA Board Meeting in Athens 2020 (text by Franziska Ylander), from the Webinar 2019 (text by Bernard Chervet), and from the EPF conference, 2016, held in Berlin (text by Jasminka Šuljagić). The chapters in Part VI, "The Vicissitudes and Maternal Function of Psychoanalytic Organisations", were presented at the IPA congress in London, 2019. Part VII, "How Do Different Societies Cope With the Disruption of Their Ideals by Wars and Covid?" is composed of texts originating from the forum organised for the EPF conference in Vienna, 2022. Part VIII, "Psychoanalytic Organisations Caught in the Crossfire", includes texts from the IPA congress held in Cartagena, 2023. The last, Part IX, "Rebirth of Psychoanalytic Organisations: Ideal and Reality Then and Now", is formed from texts presented at the IPA congress in Boston, 2020 (Franziska Ylander), and from a panel held at the EPF conference in Vienna, 2022 (Gábor Szőnyi and Christine Diercks). We would like to thank the programme committees and organisers for inviting us to present our work, and to colleagues in the audience who contributed to the discussion.

Our special thanks go to all representatives of the societies with whom we have had the opportunity to organise interviews over the previous years: the Dutch Psychoanalytical Society, Belgian Psychoanalytical Society, Argentine Psychoanalytic Association, Sao Paolo Society Brazil, Polish Psychoanalytic Society, Madrid Psychoanalytic Society, British Psychoanalytic Society, British Psychoanalytic Association, Vienna Psychoanalytic Society, Vienna Psychoanalytic Association, Hungarian Psychoanalytical Society, Colombian Psychoanalytic Society, and the Freudian Psychoanalytic Society of Colombia. We are grateful to all of them for providing us with important materials, for the in-depth discussions, and for their hospitality.

We wish to acknowledge the EPF Executive 2012–2016 for the warm and stimulating welcoming of the idea of the formation of the group on institutional matters, and to the EPF Council for the approval of the EPF Ad Hoc Institutional Matters Group (IMF) in 2015.

For those beginnings, I am grateful to Shmuel Erlich, leading the IPA Task Force on Institutional Issues at that time, for collegial support and help, as well as to Stefano Bolognini, for his inspiring thoughts about the fourth pillar for education, in the IPA Newsletter delivered to all IPA members in 2014. Many thanks to the consecutive EPF executives and for the EPF Council in 2019 for approval of the Ad Hoc Institutional Matters Group becoming the EPF Institutional Matters Forum. Our thanks also go to many colleagues whose ideas were inspirational and engaging and who have supported our work over the years in a variety of ways, one of them being participation in the IMF survey "Psychoanalytic Organisations in a Time of Crisis".

We are very grateful to the book reviewers, whose reviews were helpful in composing the book. Our very warm thanks also go to our psychoanalytic colleagues who agreed to write an endorsement, to Claudio Eizirik and to Shmuel Erlich. We are most appreciative of their work on reading the manuscript and writing endorsements.

We would also like to thank our own societies for all their work, with their varied turmoil, which have been an impetus to a wish for understanding.

Introduction

Jasminka Šuljagić

This book represents the outcome of many years of work of the Institutional Matters Forum (IMF), a working group of the European Psychoanalytical Federation consisting of seven psychoanalysts from seven different countries: Bernard Chervet (Paris Psychoanalytical Society), Christine Diercks (Vienna Psychoanalytic Society), Franziska Ylander (Swedish Psychoanalytical Association), Gábor Szőnyi (Hungarian Psychoanalytical Society), Jasminka Šuljagić (Psychoanalytical Society of Serbia), Maggiorino Genta (Swiss Psychoanalytical Society), and Philip Stokoe (British Psychoanalytic Society). Besides clinical work and publication, all group members also served in various positions within their own psychoanalytic societies and/or in European or international organisations.

We have gathered together in the need for better understanding of the turbulent life of our psychoanalytic organisations. Despite a growing interest and the literature, this wide and vague area is mostly experienced as part of our daily institutional and professional lives or retold as part of our history, marked with frequent conflicts, disruptions, splits, and impasses, but usually without the recognised space and tools for reflection. Approved at the EPF Council Meeting in October 2015 as the EPF Ad Hoc Institutional Matters Group, and in April 2019 as the EPF Forum on Institutional Matters, we set ourselves up with the aim to explore the structure, culture, and organisation of very different psychoanalytical associations, with their unique characteristics. The assumption is that this might contribute to a greater understanding of the ways in which past historical processes influence current controversies in institutional life and, hopefully, help us deal with them.

Searching for an approach to our work, we started telling each other our stories, or rather the stories of our societies, studying, listening, and reflecting on the histories of the seven societies we belong to. Differences in regions, institutional structures, histories, and other factors were revealed in considerable variety, together with some fundamental and recurring themes, mapping in this way areas for further exploration. Thereafter, we started involving and inviting other EPF societies to a joint investigation through a series of semi-structured interviews. Written historical materials are also the source of our study.

This intense learning experience includes the analysis of all collected material and many exchanges within the IMF. With very different backgrounds and

DOI: 10.4324/9781032709819-1

theoretical positions among us, but with joint curiosity and the hands-on experience of psychoanalytic institutions, we continued to maintain very open and enriching discussions. As a group that is a psychoanalytic institution as well, we also pay attention to the fact that our reflections concern our own group, making it potentially an object of our own investigation (retroactivity and après-coup).

Over time, this has been shaped into the panels and forums prepared for EPF conferences and IPA congresses, as well as for other occasions at which IMF members presented their ideas and continue to discuss them with a broader audience. Those themes revolve around the matters of legacy and origins, foundational issues, authority and identifications, group psychology, and training questions, all with their own traumatic potential and with the possibility towards the working through and transformation. Our interest has been to improve knowledge of the functioning of all institutions, linked to its aims, unconscious dynamics, and the collective psychology settled in them. Alongside this, we have also been interested in investigating the question of whether there are particularities that are unique to a psychoanalytic organisation, linked to the specificity of analytic experience and its way of transmission, that is, to the fact that our organisations consist of members who are psychoanalysts and trained within the psychoanalytic institutes.

The contributions are collected and prepared in this book, with the contents divided into nine parts.

Part I presents a starting point in thinking about psychoanalytic institutions and also a general overview of related basic concepts. The foundational issues, the theme of origins and beginnings, together with the ways in which they have been worked through and/or repeated in the subsequent histories of our institutions are investigated. The threads of individual, group, and historical truths, with their gaps, inconsistencies, and narratives, are explored, from the origins of psychoanalysis to its conception in particular psychoanalytic societies and organisations.

Part II further explores a frequent theme of our discussions, the relationship, mutual influence, and differences between the individual psyche and the functioning of groups and institutions. After delineating the realm of the infantile and its institution in the life of psychoanalytic organisations, the themes of identification and constitution of authority are outlined, with their traumatic potential and risks in work with analytic candidates. Concerning the traumatic experiences which are repressed, the question is raised of whether our psychoanalytic institutions are sometimes used to finding communities of denial and to warding off feelings of lack.

Part III at first takes a closer look at our group's working method and the complex dynamics of different registers, each of them expressing a conflict between two desires: to be different from others (to be one of a kind) and to be like others (to be one among others). This is followed by a consideration of similar conflictual dualities, keeping others and separating/differentiating from them, where the life of the group is the scene for reviving both. Various snapshots from the lives of our psychoanalytical organisations are presented, as well as the tendency to "use psychoanalytical concepts defensively" in group situations/institutions. Finally, ways of using psychoanalytic concepts in a constructive and helpful way to understand organisational dynamics are developed.

Part IV concerns the sense of intimacy in a group and organisational life, especially the life in our psychoanalytic institutions, with their unique characteristics and close connection with the work of intimacy in an analytic setting. Various changes and modalities are followed and explored. The conditions and protocol of the sessions of psychoanalysis allow the spaces and paths of intimacy for each subject, while the constitution of the organisation, with the necessity for organised structure and rules, as well as with transference of authority, places the fate of intimacy into a delicate and challenging balance within a group and organisational life. Regarding training regulations and procedures for accreditation, several questions are raised. Does not the institutional space, which should remain both supple and regulated at the same time, sometimes have a tendency to become rigid, especially in older societies? Is there something about the intimacy of the psychoanalytic engagement with the patient that creates a resistance against the development of a managed, hierarchical organisation, and does a sense of intimacy appear to be threatened by a more organised structure?

Following the questions of origin, differentiation, the infantile, and intimacy in the previous parts, Part V turns once again to some of the key topics in the realm of institutional matters: the concept of authority in psychoanalytical institutions, the impact of the society for the individual psychoanalyst, and a question of transmission of psychoanalysis. Different determinations of the concept of authority are presented: investigation of its contemporary fate and its place in different phases of the psychoanalysis and psychoanalytic organisations. Excerpts from the institutional history are used, with motifs from literature, mythology, and sociology, all in an attempt of its understanding through the prism of the metapsychological theory. The concepts of violence and denial are emphasised as inevitable for the thinking on psychoanalytic institutions. Regarding the impact of the society for the individual psychoanalyst, a sketch of currently present conflicts and problem areas in the functioning of psychoanalytical institutions is given. This is followed by the reflections on the models of training and on the French model in particular, proposing that any training is not only a place for the transfer of authority but also of negative tendencies, which have consequences on our capacity to become and re-become analysts and on our institutional functioning.

Part VI presents different approaches to psychoanalytic organisations. One of them is a developmental one, describing the birth, developmental stages, and pitfalls of newborn societies (the feeling of otherness, the faces of fears from and for the organisation, the repetition of early conflict patterns, and the capacity to split), based on the experience we gained, especially from tutorial work with newborn, developing analytic societies in Eastern Europe. The other approach deals with its underlying features, exploring the maternal function in its two forms: "the maternal as an unknown source" and "a conflict between maternal function and Oedipal structuring". Both approaches make connections with training and with the life of the analytic candidates.

Part VII includes two texts on everlasting and urgent issues, wars and the Covid-19 pandemic. The title was applied as a headline for the setting of a forum situation where, during EPF conference, members of the EPF came together to discuss and share both recent and old experiences. Initiating open and free discussions on matters like this, matters of great sensitivity, seemed important to heighten awareness of institutional matters among members of the psychoanalytic community and to find ways to navigate through situations of threat and loss on the level of psychoanalytical societies.

Part VIII presents the continuation of a consideration of contemporary issues in the life of psychoanalytic organisations, with an emphasis on "psychoanalytic organisations caught in the crossfire", and on matters of collective psychology, group mentality, and mass psychology. The great traumas of history have had major effects on our organisations, their interruptions, their disappearances, and their rebirths. History, therefore, contains determinants that we, at the Institutional Matter Forum, are trying to identify and which play a part in multifactorial overdetermination. The singular personal dynamics of a psyche, organised by an oscillatory interplay between daytime and night-time activities, between sleeping-dreaming and social life, between work and eroticism, has no equivalent in group dynamics. This part also involves the survey report, another approach to our work. The survey consisted of five questions about the major internal crisis/crises that the societies have gone through in their histories, as well as the impact of major global crises: World War II, the Covid-19 crisis, the war in Ukraine, and an open question about other crises and their impact.

Part IX is about the central topic of our book, reflected on in all the previous parts, about the rebirth of psychoanalytic organisations and "ideal and reality then and now". Here, this is exemplified by the challenges and transformations of the Vienna Psychoanalytic Society and the Hungarian Psychoanalytic Society. This part also addresses the splitting of two societies in the 1960s and the work towards merging again as the Swedish Psychoanalytic Association *in the 2010s*. It includes important observations from a follow-up study made two years after the fusion.

All those parts, taken together, present the evolving thinking of the Institutional Matters Forum. Through our joint work, a space has been opened for reflection and dialogue on the matters of importance for the life of our psychoanalytic organisations. It was recognised and valued by our colleagues at our forums and panels, and we wish the same for our readers.

Part I

On the Origin of
Psychoanalytic Organisations

Chapter 1

On the Origin of Psychoanalytic Institutions in Vienna

Christine Diercks

The IMG group has started thinking about institutional matters and is discussing our specific foundation issues being repeated in the subsequent histories of our institutions – thereby interfering with the experience of beginning in each new generation. Coming from Vienna, I will share with you some of my thoughts about aspects of the history of the Vienna Psychoanalytic Society,[1] the beginning of its institutionalisation and systematic psychoanalytic training; but because of the privileged position of our society in early times, this is about the founding issues of all our institutions too.

Origin

Though "it did not drop from the skies ready-made",[2] *psychoanalysis* is the creation of Sigmund Freud. On his way to providing a psychology based in natural science, an inner world opened up to him, which cannot be reduced to a copy or simple reaction to the external world but which follows its own laws and drives, and this exposes us to inner conflicts which are in complex interplay with the external reality. Freud's method was revolutionary and made accessible a field of scientific enquiry which would have otherwise been impossible to research: the unconscious and infant sexuality. Something new had been introduced, something which re-examined Western culture and established an independent scientific method which Freud went on to call psychoanalysis as early as 1896.

Despite substantial critique and hostilities, the new science and its methods were to receive significant recognition. Without exception, the first who felt themselves drawn to Freud's new ideas were of Jewish descent; they helped create a productive atmosphere amendable to experimentation extending beyond social and academic conventions and which was required for the further investigation of this new dimension of thought. They started to meet with Freud regularly on Wednesdays in Berggasse 19 in 1902. The group quickly grew, and emerging from this legendary Wednesday society, in 1908, the Viennese Psychoanalytic Society was constituted for the "nurture and advancement of the psychoanalytic science founded by Prof. Dr. Sigmund Freud in Vienna", as can still be read today in our society's by-laws.

DOI: 10.4324/9781032709819-3

International Recognition

Personal contact with Eugen Bleuler, C. G. Jung, and a group of visiting doctors, such as Karl Abraham, A. A. Brill, Max Eitingon, Ernest Jones, and Herman Nunberg, at the University of Zurich, at that time an international stronghold of academic psychiatry and psychotherapy, opened the door to the world for Freud's psychoanalysis. "In the Burgholzli we are zealous admirers of Freud's theories in psychology and pathology" (letter, Bleuler to Freud, 21 September 1904).[3] The exchange of letters was followed by visits; a first meeting of Freudian psychoanalysis in 1908 in Salzburg established the tradition of the international psychoanalytic congresses, and in 1909 Freud, Jung, and Sándor Ferenczi travelled to the USA. Based on the model of the Vienna Society, local psychoanalytic groups were founded in Europe and New York, which merged in 1910 under the umbrella of an International Psychoanalytic Association. Only Bleuler refused membership. For him, science was not a matter of a private association but of a public university.

Freud placed great hope in Jung, whom he appreciated as a "Christian and pastor's son", and subscribed to his theory, hoping that "psychoanalysis was safe from the danger . . . of becoming a Jewish national affair", as he wrote in a private letter to Abraham in 1908 (letter, Freud to Abraham, 01 May 1908).[4]

Struggling for scientific recognition and an appropriate place in the public eye, Freud urged Jung as early as 1907 to found his own psychoanalytic journal. Jung expressed first ideas, and the enthusiastic Freud answered, "What magnificent plans! . . . To tell the truth, your plans for the journal please me even more, that is a matter of life or death for our ideas" (Freud to Jung, 21 December 1907).[5] In 1909, they published the first volume of the *Jahrbuch für psychoanalytische und psychopathologische Forschung*, directed by Bleuler and Freud, edited by Jung, who also became the first president of the IPA in 1910. Freud preferred him to the members of the Vienna group, among which were his oldest and most loyal followers, a fact that caused embittered responses among some.

The "Viennese", above all, Alfred Adler and Wilhelm Stekel, felt neglected by Jung's appointment as editor of the yearbook and president of the IPA. As a compensation, Alfred Adler became chairman of the Vienna Psychoanalytic Society in 1910, and a second psychoanalytic journal, the *Zentralblatt*, located in Vienna, was founded, directed by Freud, edited by Adler and Stekel, the first issue of which was published in 1911.

But the secession turned out to be impossible to prevent, and Adler and his followers left the WPV the same year. This was later followed by a break between Freud and Jung in 1914.

Freud finally gave up the *Jahrbuch* and the *Zentralblatt*. He founded two other journals: in 1912, the *IMAGO, Zeitschrift für Anwendung der Psychoanalyse auf die Geisteswissenschaften*, directed by Freud, edited by Otto Rank und Hanns Sachs, and instead of the *Zentralblatt*, the *Internationale Zeitschrift für [ärztliche] Psychoanalyse*, also directed by Freud and edited by Ferenczi and Rank, was first released in 1913.

Despite these crises, psychoanalysis was in the process of making its break-through not only in Vienna but also internationally. This development was to come to an abrupt halt with the outbreak of WWI.

Psychoanalytic Training and Clinics

The end of the war brought many upheavals and new foundations. The psychoanalysts finally met again at the International Congress of Psychoanalysis in Budapest in 1918: Freud raised the prospect for the establishment of a psychoanalytic publishing house, which was founded in 1919. And Freud campaigned for psychoanalytic clinics offering treatment for patients without means. Nunberg made demands for establishing preparatory analysis for future analysts and specialised training programs.

As a consequence, the Berlin Polyclinic, established mainly by Eitingon, opened its doors in 1920, not only offering treatment for poor people, but also providing a model and an institution for systematic psychoanalytic training. This is until today known as the Eitingon model, consisting of a personal analysis, theoretical and clinical seminars, and training analysis of patients under supervision – which is still the training model of the Vienna Psychoanalytic Society today.

A similar clinic for psychoanalysis, the "Ambulatorium" (free clinic), was founded in Vienna in 1922, initiated by Eduard Hitschmann as well as Helene and Felix Deutsch. Due to the fact that Austrian law only allowed treatment of patients by medical doctors, training tasks were separated from the psychoanalytic work in the clinic, directed by Hitschmann, and an independent institute for training was founded in 1925, which was open also for "lay" analysts, directed by Helene Deutsch.

Establishing the training program changed a lot.

In the early times, access to the meetings of the Vienna Psychoanalytic Society was given by personal invitation. After presenting a paper, one could become a member; it was not a condition to get trained or to practice psychoanalysis. Not only doctors were welcome but also, as Freud (1914) remembered, "the circle included others – men of education who had recognized something important in psycho-analysis: writers, painters and so on".[6] The early members brought with them the most diverse academic qualifications. Amongst them were also "eccentrics, dreamers and sensitive dispositions" who, as Anna Freud[7] put it later, felt themselves drawn to Freud's new ideas and helped create the productive, experimental atmosphere beyond social and academic conventions which was required for the further investigation of this new dimension of thought.

Already before WWI, the WPV started with introduction lectures to psychoanalysis, and also, courses in psychoanalysis for physician, for students of all faculties, for the women's education association, and even for judges and state prosecutors were offered. Later personal analysis for future analysts was suggested, and in 1920, the first training institute started its work in the Berlin Polyclinic, followed by the Vienna Ambulatorium. Finally, at the IPA congress in Bad

Homburg in 1925, Eitingon introduced his "training guidelines" – the "Eitingon model" – and founded the International Training Commission. Training should no longer be left to the private initiative but must be organised and authorised by collective responsibility.

The IPA was founded as a scientific association. Initially, membership in the IPA did not require training and practice of psychoanalysis. But from 1925, only those could become members of the IPA who have completed the entire clinical training program, which had to follow the rules of the IPA. As a result, the IPA changed from a scientific association into a more professional organisation of psychoanalysts. The IPA regulations for education became the gatekeeper for membership.

This was a substantial change with many consequences and conflicts. The first one about lay analysis started immediately: already in 1925, Clarence Oberndorfer presented the position of the American groups (APA) to exclude non-physicians from training.[8] Freud (1926) was strongly opposed to the monopolisation of psychoanalysis by medicine and published *Zur Frage der Laienanalyse*[9] (*Question of Lay Analysis*). He claimed that the IPA should no longer be an administrative and executive body but instead an informal affiliation of local associations which organised scientific activities. IPA committees and commissions tried to solve this conflict, and finally, according to a gentleman's agreement, the IPA was no longer responsible for training in the USA.

The new international regulations had the very important – and, in many ways, indispensable – function to obtain a high standard of training and to protect the basic assumption of psychoanalysis. But if we still understand psychoanalysis not only as "a method for the treatment" but also as a method "for the investigation of mental processes, which are almost inaccessible in any other way" and as "a collection of psychological information obtained along those lines, which is gradually being accumulated into a new scientific discipline" (Freud, 1923/1922, p. 235),[10] then we need appropriate structures to provide academic culture and interdisciplinary exchange and research.

These are challenges that still concern us today.

New Generation

Wilhelm Reich became the first assistant at the "Ambulatorium" (free clinic) in November 1923. At that time, while the foundations of psychoanalytic treatment techniques were already established, practice still lagged behind. Like all his young colleagues in great technical straits, Reich, always on the go, encouraged the establishment of a therapeutic-technical seminar, which he then himself led from 1924 until 1930. An entire generation of analysts was indebted to this seminar for the fundamental aspects of treatment technique, resistance and character analysis, and with Reich's broadened concept of transference, a deeper understanding in dealing with negative transference.

Like Wilhelm Reich, many of the young analysts were involved in left-wing youth movements: Siegfried Bernfeld, Grete and Edward Bibring, Otto Fenichel,

Willi Hoffer, Anni Reich. Critical of culture and society, they campaigned for sexual education, school reform, and national adult education programs and applied psychoanalysis to these areas. August Aichhorn was the head of educational advisory centres. Anna Freud developed her model of child analysis. The Society offered very well-attended seminars for kindergarten and schoolteachers.

This second generation of analysts encountered a quite different psychoanalysis from that of the first pioneers 20 years earlier who, in part, had not gone through these great upheavals. With *Beyond the Pleasure Principle* (Freud, 1920) and the introduction of the psychic structures of the ego, id, and superego (Freud, 1923), Freud once more substantially extended psychoanalysis. One person who had eagerly taken up these new ideas was Melanie Klein, also Viennese-born but, at this time, already working in Berlin, who broke new ground in the research on early infancy and who, by entering this field, was in direct competition with Anna Freud. Owing to the different scientific approaches, far-reaching tensions between the groups from Vienna and London, where Melanie Klein now lived and worked, began to develop. Therefore, an exchange of lectures was established between the Vienna and the British Society.

The Persecution of Jewish Analysts and the End of Psychoanalysis in Vienna in 1938

In Germany, Jewish analysts were persecuted since 1933, and some of them moved to Vienna. But the dominant Austrofascism, which had assumed power in Austria since 1934, also led to initial emigration and made those remaining behind in Vienna remain silent. The National Socialists' rise to power signified the end of psychoanalysis in Vienna and the Vienna Society with its institutions (clinic, training institute, and the publishing house). On 13 March 1938, a board meeting was held, and two resolutions were passed: that all members should flee the country as soon as possible, and that the seat of the Society was to be relocated to wherever Freud would take up residence.

Not all the society members and candidates succeeded in fleeing from the Nazis. Rosa Walk probably jumped out of the window so as not to be arrested by the Gestapo in Paris. Alfred Bass, Adolf Deutsch, Margarethe Hilferding, Salomea Kempner, Karl Landauer, Alfred Meisl, David Ernst Oppenheim, Isidor Sadger, Sabina Spielrein, and Nikola Sugar were all murdered. They were members of the Vienna Psychoanalytic Society who had not lived in Vienna for a long time or who had left the group before 1938. What happened to the candidates is still subject of research being done by members of the Vienna Society.

London became the new centre of psychoanalysis, as Freud and his family, along with several Viennese analysts, had been granted asylum there.

Thus, the scientific conflict between London and Vienna was transferred to the British Society, where it escalated and went down in the history of psychoanalysis as "controversial discussions" (the Freud–Klein controversy). Freud's death in 1939, the question as to who should succeed him, and the existential threat looming over the whole of Europe contributed to the vehemence with which this debate was conducted; the consequences, however, were to become entirely productive.

During this period, psychoanalysis was expelled from Vienna but spread considerably in Anglo-American countries, and the immigrants from continental Europe contributed substantially to this development.

Notes

1 See Diercks (2008); Diercks & Ruhs (2020).
2 See Sigmund Freud (1924), SE 19:191.
3 See Schröter, 2012.
4 See Falzeder & Hermanns, 2009.
5 See McGuire (1974).
6 See Sigmund Freud (1914).
7 See Anna Freud (1969).
8 From 1938, on this APA position that severe consequences for Jewish refugees from Europe not being medical doctors. Finally, the IPA offered them direct IPA membership.
9 See Sigmund Freud (1926).
10 "Psycho-Analysis is the name (1) of a procedure for the investigation of mental processes which are almost inaccessible in any other way, (2) of a method (based upon that investigation) for the treatment of neurotic disorders and (3) of a collection of psychological information obtained along those lines, which is gradually being accumulated into a new scientific discipline." (Freud, 1923/1922, GW 13:211; SE 18:235).

References

Diercks, C. (2008). Dis-continuity. *Psychoanalysis in Europe, Bulletin, 62*, 11–16. European Psychoanalytic Federation.
Diercks, C., & Ruhs, A. (2020). Letter from Vienna. *International Journal of Psychoanalysis, 101*(3), 589–594.
Falzeder, E., & Hermanns, L. (Ed.). (2009). *Sigmund Freud/Karl Abraham. Briefwechsel 1907–1925. Band 1*. Turia + Kant, Verlag; Neuauflage.
Freud, S. (1914). *Zur Geschichte der psychoanalytischen Bewegung. GW* (Vol. 10, p. 63); *On the history of the psycho-analytic movement. SE* (Vol. 14, p. 26).
Freud, S. (1920). *Jenseits des Lustprinzips. GW* (Vol. 13, pp. 3–69); *Beyond the pleasure principle. SE* (Vol. 18, pp. 1–64).
Freud, S. (1923). *Psychoanalyse und libidotheorie. GW* (Vol. 13, p. 211); *Psychoanalysis. SE* (Vol. 18, p. 235). (Original work published 1922)
Freud, S. (1923). *Das Ich und das Es. GW* (Vol. 13, pp. 237–289); *The ego and the Id. SE* (Vol. 19, pp. 12–59).
Freud, S. (1924). *Kurzer Abriss der Psychoanalyse. GW* (Vol. 13, pp. 403–427); *A short account of psycho-analysis. SE* (Vol. 19, pp. 191–209).
Freud, S. (1926). *Die Frage der Laienanalyse. GW* (Vol. 14, pp. 209–263); *The question of lay analysis. SE* (Vol. 20, pp. 177–258).
Freud, A. (1987). Schwierigkeiten der Psychoanalyse in Vergangenheit und Gegenwart. In *Die Schriften der Anna Freud* (Vol. I, pp. 2481–2508). (Original work published 1969)
McGuire, W. (1974). *The Freud/Jung letters*. University Press.
Schröter, M. (Ed.). (2012). *Sigmund Freud – Eugen Bleuler. Briefwechsel 1907–1937*. Schwabe.

Chapter 2

The Origin of Psychoanalytic Institutions and Their Compulsion to Repeat

Some Thoughts

Philip Stokoe

This brief chapter derives from the material that our group has been investigating. The theoretical models originate not only in straightforward psychoanalytic theory but also from the psychoanalytic and systemic understanding of groups and organisations developed over 70 years at the Tavistock Institute of Human Relations and the Tavistock Clinic.

I shall begin by describing some crucial concepts of organisational good function so that I can apply those theories to the common experience of psychoanalytic institutions that we have been looking at and which have been written about by other colleagues.

Entrepreneurial or Managed Hierarchy

Amongst all the other things that can be said about Freud, he was an entrepreneur; he had an idea which he built upon to create an organisation. The thoughts that I shall be offering today are that the origins of the psychoanalytic organisation have been repeated like a repetition compulsion to the detriment of the development of psychoanalytic institutions.

In my work as an organisational consultant, I have very frequently been called in to help organisations that were created by a single individual (or sometimes a small group) to change their style into a managed hierarchy. I am using the expression "managed hierarchy" to describe the normal shape of successful organisations across the world. In such organisations, tasks are carried out to achieve the organisation's main purpose by individuals who have been authorised to make decisions and act in pursuit of those aims by somebody to whom they report who has also been authorised in a similar fashion. The arrangement of authorisation and account is contained by an executive team, often called directors, who report directly to a chief executive. The chief executive is authorised to make decisions on behalf of the main purpose of the group or organisation by a board who is responsible for the governance of their system and for setting the strategic direction.

In my experience, the move from the entrepreneurial arrangement to a managed hierarchy is resisted very strongly by the organisation, even when individuals within that organisation all agree that it is the best thing. The Tavistock approach to understanding organisations is based upon the assumption that processes which might be

DOI: 10.4324/9781032709819-4

described as a group or organisational unconscious, like the individual unconscious, operate to avoid anxiety and set up defensive structures to achieve that end.

The entrepreneurial organisation is shaped like a spider's web. At the centre is the father or mother, but all the individuals working for the organisation are connected directly to the centre by their own thread. Thus, everybody feels equally important, and there is an experience of linkage to the centre that matches very much Freud's description of groups with leaders in his *Group Psychology and the Analysis of the Ego*. It is easy to see how difficult the workers will find it to let go of this direct access to the mother/father and report instead to somebody who appears to be an intermediary.

At the EPF conference in 2016, Jasminka Šuljagić presented a paper describing the difficulty that Freud experienced in moving from a meeting in "the professor's study" to the beginning of a psychoanalytic organisation. His colleagues simply did not want to move from the cosiness of a gathering around "the Professor", which would be the first step toward a managed system and away from the entrepreneurial gathering.

As you will have guessed, my suggestion is that there is something very primitive about an arrangement where everybody has direct access to the main person; I have already used parental figures to express this. I don't think anybody would disagree that Wilfred Bion's description of the defensive organisation of a group that he called "basic assumption dependence" (Bion, 1961) matches exactly what Freud was describing in group psychology. Sometimes the defensive structures are actually helpful because of the particular nature of the problem faced by the group. It is useful that an army can move between basic assumption dependence and basic assumption fight/flight because of the extraordinary nature of their predicament, which is that they are actually in conflict with other human beings and their lives are in danger. This is not the case in psychoanalytic institutions. Although sometimes our group has heard stories that would suggest that people really have believed that they are under terrifying threat from other psychoanalysts. I am suggesting that the feeling of threat and the intensity of that feeling derived from the nature of a change from the comforting position of the nursery to a grown-up position in the real world.

At this point, I want to draw attention to a feature that accompanies dysfunction in an organisation. It is implied in what I have just said, and it is described very clearly by writers like Bion and Jaques; when an organisation or a group becomes caught up in a defensive structure, its attention is taken directly from the outside into itself. It is one of the signatures that an organisational consultant looks for in attempting to understand problems in such a setting, namely, that people have become preoccupied with each other. Everything feels personal. This does not mean that every individual is feeling something at a personal level all the time; what it does mean is that some people feel that things are about personalities, or they feel that they are personally being mistreated.

Tasks and Restrictions

I would be surprised if anybody disagreed that a central feature of adult functioning is the capacity to face reality. In contrast to those defensive structures that he described as basic assumption modes, Bion saw it as one of the main features of a "working group" that it would be able to face reality in two particular forms. The first would be the reality of the task facing the group, and the second would be the reality of the resources available from within the group to achieve that task. Elliott Jaques observed such structures at work when he was studying industrial relations in the glazier metalwork factory run by Wilfred Brown. He gave them the name "social systems as a defence against anxiety" (Jaques, 1951, 1955).

In the psychoanalytic approach to understanding organisations, a very important feature is the main or primary task of that organisation. This concept of primary task has been a diagnostic indicator for dysfunction for those of us working with organisations; it is not too much of an exaggeration to say that in very dysfunctional organisations there are as many conceptualisations of the primary task as there are individuals at work. Putting it the other way around, a healthy organisation is one whose mission statement (which is the modern term for primary task) is clear and known by everybody in the organisation. It is also a mark of a healthy organisation that it is constantly reviewing the relevance of its primary task. Today's primary task might well be tomorrow's piece of history. The other example of dysfunctional attitude to primary task is when that organisational aim becomes so idealised that it cannot be questioned. Once again, this has been a feature of some of the descriptions of psychoanalytic institutions in crisis.

The question about the primary task is not only whether it remains relevant; very often, there appear to be competing primary tasks. Pierre Turquet, another of the founding members of the Tavistock approach, gave a very good example of how important it is to be clear, which is the ultimate primary task. He asked the question about a teaching hospital: Is the primary task to teach or to treat? Then he produced an example to clarify the issue: An operation is being carried out by the consultant surgeon in front of students. Suddenly, the patient starts to haemorrhage. Clearly, if the primary task is teaching, this is an ideal opportunity for the consultant to step back and ask if anybody has any ideas. In other words, it is pretty obvious that the primary task is treatment, and that education is a subsidiary task. Once again, I make this point in the full awareness that many psychoanalytic institutions have come into serious internal conflict around issues of training.

Just as important as clarity about the primary task for keeping an organisation healthy is clarity about the parameters within which the organisation can operate. Obviously, the financial constraints that arise from the organisation's working budget will be very important, but there are other parameters that apply. I am thinking most particularly about ethical considerations. In a factory, the transformation of steel plate into dustbins will attract very little ethical concern; it does not matter if you hit the steel in order to make it take up the shape that you want. When your task involves working with other human beings, it really does matter whether there is an organisational attitude to hitting or taking any other physical action towards them. The Hippocratic oath that governs medical organisations certainly applies to psychoanalytic institutions, but there are others as well.

If the primary task of a psychoanalytic institution is to propagate and develop psychoanalytic ideas, how it goes about its business should be a model of applying those ideas. I have already hinted that it is normal for organisations to be driven by an unconscious wish to avoid anxiety. It is easy to see that the individuals in organisations will become recruited on behalf of such defences at an unconscious level. Now we have a problem as psychoanalysts, which is that we tend to believe that our analysis makes us less available to unconscious dynamics. I think this is a very dangerous assumption. I would suggest that one of the parameters that all psychoanalytic institutions ought to hold highly is the recognition that individuals *inevitably* will get caught up in defensive organisational dynamics, and so it would be sensible for the organisation to provide mechanisms for recognising these processes and turning actions into meaningful insights.

You may be surprised to hear that the best-functioning commercial organisations apply this approach without necessarily even realising they are doing so. It is done by providing oversight of the organisation's compliance with the parameters that I have been discussing. This is generally called governance and is the role allocated to the board that is responsible for that organisation. Boards appoint chief executives to appoint a workforce and carry out the necessary work to achieve the aims that the board has agreed for that organisation. The chief executive accounts to the board, which has the duty to interrogate the activities of the workforce against the parameters that have been agreed. When this duty is carried out with benign interest rather than persecutory micromanagement, it has the merit that it notices pressures to move away from agreed parameters and, by exploring those pressures, can usually learn important information about the underlying anxieties picked up by the workforce.

To put it succinctly, a healthy organisation must separate the functions of governance from those of managing the work. Where they become merged, there will always be a collapse into more primitive functioning.

Repetition of the Origin

To return to the beginning, when Freud decided to move out of his study and instate the process that would lead to the IPA and the process of bringing psychoanalytic ideas to the rest of the world, he immediately encountered two problems. The first was the resistance of his colleagues to such a move. It might well be that Freud suffered as much as everybody else did from the consequence of being caught up in a defensive system that I described earlier on, namely, that it felt personal. I am suggesting this because of the interesting phenomenon that followed a little bit later, which was the development of the secret society, signified by rings that Freud gave to his inner circle (see Grosskurth, 1991). Very often, inner circles are created because the feeling that we are amongst enemies is so convincing that nobody questions it. I am suggesting that these sorts of feelings *must* be questioned and questioned from a position that we are actually rather good at doing when we have these experiences in the consulting room. In our work with patients, we fully expect to be filled with different sorts of feelings, and so it is part of our good practice always to ask the question: What does this feeling mean, and to whom does it really belong? I think it is such a shock to discover that not only do we have our own unconscious but also, as soon as we are in a group, we are subject to a phenomenon that might be described as a group unconscious.

It has become my view since studying psychoanalytic institutions that we suffer from a problem that is unique; we have an extremely deep and well-tested understanding of the individual unconscious. The reason this is a problem is the phenomenon by which institutional dynamics always make the individuals involved focus on the other individuals rather than the larger picture of the organisation. The way that this manifests itself in our institutions is that people appear to make comments about the institutional problem by referring to what I can only describe as an analogy to individual unconscious functioning. A good example of this – and I am afraid that there are many such examples – is the number of times that I have been told by colleagues that their institution, or some other psychoanalytic institution that they have been told about, exhibits issues that are clearly of an Oedipal origin. I have to tell you that, in over 30 years of consulting to organisations, I have never once encountered an organisation whose problems were Oedipal. I have, however, very often encountered organisations that would like to convince me that the reason everything is in a mess is the uncontrollable rivalrous feelings in other people. Perhaps you will anticipate what I am going to say about that, namely, that it is only when those apparent rivalries are understood in terms of the organisational anxieties that you can get a proper picture of the situation, and it never *originates* with an individual's rivalling feelings towards another.[1]

Freud's second problem, which might have been the reason that he wanted to move out of his study, was the challenge of how to train more people to become psychoanalysts. As we all know, Freud believed that academic institutions would not be prepared to provide a place for psychoanalytic training because they would dismiss it as Jewish and the intrinsic antisemitism in those institutions would make it impossible to set up trainings where, I think, he would have preferred them to be. Instead, it became necessary to develop trainings within psychoanalytic institutions.

So the features that I believe were central to the origin of psychoanalytic institutions were, firstly, that psychoanalysis was the invention of one man who attracted like-minded people to him and, in that way, developed an entrepreneurial embryonic organisation. Secondly, that the birth of psychoanalytic institutions required the move away from the sojourn in the maternal/paternal breast directly to an adult state of functioning in which direct access to that parent would no longer be possible. To be fair, in normal human development, this is not such a direct step; there is the extreme chaos and disturbance of adolescence that contains all the anxieties about taking up an adult position. Thirdly, one of the driving forces was the need to create new psychoanalysts, and this process was contaminated by the idea that this form of education would be unwelcome in academic circles. In other words, part of the aim of the neonate psychoanalytic institution, to teach others, was immediately associated with a sense of challenge and denigration (remember, the source was antisemitic). I do not think you have to be a psychoanalyst to guess that the reaction against this kind of underlying belief would be retaliatory and that the retaliation would be in the form of idealising the training that was to be created. It should therefore be no surprise to any of us studying our institutions that arguments centre on the question of the "pure gold" of the psychoanalytic training being in some way threatened by contamination from outside.

My suggestion is that the wish to return to an entrepreneurial system repeats itself time and again in institutions in the form of arguments about theory or practice. If we can distance ourselves from the content of these arguments, it becomes blindingly obvious that the institutional consequence is to form smaller circles around apparently contested ideas. In other words, at the point at which the institution needs to become grown-up about difference, there is a regression to a small group centred on a maternal or paternal figure.

The repetition compulsion is further demonstrated in the preoccupation with training. Freud did not set up the institutions simply to be places to train psychoanalysis; he wanted to bring psychoanalysis and psychoanalytic ideas to the wider world. It is rare for psychoanalytic institutions to recognise, using Turquet's test, that the primary task is to bring psychoanalytic ideas to the world and the education of psychoanalysts is a subsidiary task. Instead, the institution acts out an idea that someone somewhere is challenging the pure gold that is the psychoanalytic training. The entire system becomes consumed with this inward struggle, whilst the external world continues separately. There cannot be a better illustration of this than the so-called "controversial discussions" of my own society in the middle of the Second World War!

Note

1 One of the reasons that people assume that problems arise with a particular individua is another of Bion's concepts, "valency". These days, we would say that our personal vulnerabilities, often manifesting as personality traits, offer something like an unconscious hook onto which patients and institutions can project unwanted emotions or beliefs. Thus, someone with a particular "hook" is unconsciously chosen over and over to express a particular feeling or view, thereby lending credibility to the theory that these arise in that person rather than are channelled through him.

References

Bion, W. R. (1989). *Experiences in groups* (pp. 116–117). Tavistock Publications. (Reprinted from Routledge, 1961)

Grosskurth, P. (1991). *The secret ring; Freud's inner circle and the politics of psychoanalysis*. Addison-Wesley Publishing Company.

Jaques, E. (1951). *The changing culture of a factory; A study of authority and participation in an industrial setting*. Routledge & Kegan Paul Ltd.

Jaques, E. (1955). Social systems as a defence against persecutory and depressive anxiety. In *New directions in psycho-analysis*. Tavistock Publications & Basic Books.

Šuljagić, J. (2016). *The many facets of authority in psychoanalytic institutions*. EPF Conference.

Part II

Infantile and Institutionalisation

Chapter 3

The Role of the Infantile and Its Shortcomings in Institutional Events

Bernard Chervet

Psychoanalysts have always been interested in the functioning of their own institutions inasmuch as they have their origins, like all institutions of our civilisation, in the needs of human beings.

Multiple observations have been made with attempts to interpret the group functioning that governs them, either by applying certain individual psychic mechanisms transposed onto the group or, on the contrary, by means of concepts derived from other fields, such as sociology, economics, management, or anthropology.

In our work group, we have often expressed reservations concerning the application of individual psychology to group phenomena. Nonetheless, we cannot overlook the fact that the latter appear to be overdetermined by unconscious psychic motives and processes that are found to be operative during sessions, such as the Oedipus complex, the murder of the father, incestuous dynamics, repression, the conflict between patriarchal and fraternal logics, the requirements of spiritualisation related to an idea, anti-traumatic or self-calming mechanisms, and so on.

The point of view that would involve a conceptualisation arising from another field to throw light on group functioning with its intelligibility is not satisfying either, owing to the fact that it does not involve the psychic factor.

Admittedly, it is important not to confuse individual functioning and group functioning, which does not have the possibility each night of realising a formal regression and hallucinatory wish fulfilment, except by pursuing an animistic logic which treats the group as a being as such, endowed with an unconscious, formal regressive possibilities, dreamwork, and a capacity for libidinal regeneration. The history of civilisations shows that this is not the case and that civilisations undergo ruptures and fractures, even collapses and disappearances, rather than sleep and dream cycles with creative and generative libidinal regeneration.

Managing to remain close to the psyche and its unconscious modes of functioning, while maintaining a differentiation between intrapsychic events and intra-group events, seems to me to be a challenge that merits discussion.

One path presents itself to us, namely, the emergence of the psyche. In order to deploy itself, the potential psyche is transposed onto an operative psyche. It can thus identify with it. The primary mechanism of transposition, which is so valuable for analysts in terms of transference, remains an enigma.

DOI: 10.4324/9781032709819-6

Transposition and identification are at the basis of the individual psyche. They are the reminiscences involved in group psychologies. The emergence of the psyche requires the mental and physical presence of another human being, a *Nebenmensch*, as an object of satisfaction, as an object of hostility, as a model and helping power. The interplay of presence–absence (*Fort-Da*) is at the origin of very differentiated modalities of psychic work, which are all indispensable. This is true for the following situations familiar to every child with these others who offer their presence–absence to permit his or her growth: physically present, mentally absent; physically absent, mentally present; perception of lack in situations of presence and absence; feelings of lack in situations of absence and presence; etc.

As a result, collective psychology is an integral part of individual psychology, but with a particularity. The aspects that make up group or collective psychology or group mentality or mass psychology are components of individual psychology which can only be expressed through a group or a mass. They can therefore be the object of our analytic work during sessions. But intervening in such functioning at the level of groups is another matter.

Some psychoanalysts think that it is preferable to give up the use of interpretation when treating a group in difficulty, and to help the group overcome the difficulty by re-cathecting its major objectives. They then propose enlightened forms of management related to a conception of ideal institutional functioning.

My choice is to continue to elaborate the individual potentialities that can only be expressed through a group potentialisation. An individual may turn out to be a serial murderer, but a genocide can only be perpetrated by a massification of an individual potentiality that is only realised within a group.

The foundational identification contains such potentialities, but a second identification is necessary between the group members themselves and with the same aim so that these potentialities can manifest themselves. The group members must be guided by the same purpose that takes the form of an ideal; in the case of genocides, it is the belief that it is possible to eliminate the individual traumatic dimension by eradicating a part of reality perceivable through sensoriality.

It was by studying hallucinatory wish fulfilment that Freud made his entry into collective psychology, in connection with the phenomenon of contagiousness between several people. An affective tie is established between them based on the fact that they have the same unconscious wishes in common. Their daytime relations make it possible to fulfil this wish in a concealed way. The concealment is based on this group tie. During dreams, the censorship guarantees the concealment. During the day, it is the group tie that supports repression.

Freud introduced the notion of psychic contagiousness by means of a hysterical identification. It was in the *Traumdeutung* that he discovered this form of identification by studying a key dream that has become very famous, *the dream of the butcher's wife* (in French, *le rêve du repas manqué* [dream of the missed meal]) (Freud, 1900, pp. 147–149), a dream that has been copiously commented on in the psychoanalytic literature and, in France, by Lacan. Under Lacan's pen, this dream became the *dream of the beautiful butcher's wife*.

It is worth noting that this change of name participates fully in the collective concealment, whereas the title given by Freud was the beginning of an interpretation. The lack of manifest content relates to the failure to give up the satisfaction of Oedipal desires. The hysterical identification concerns two women friends, one of whom had the famous dream. Freud directed his attention to a common point between them and not to the dreamer's psyche alone. The common point consisted in depriving each other of the offers of their respective husbands, in one case the salmon, and in the other the caviar.

His interpretation of this deprivation concerned their Oedipal desire towards their respective fathers, a generic Oedipal desire which they both had in common.

Contagiousness was at the origin of a relationship based on a desexualised homosexuality between two women friends. It concerned their Oedipal desire and the obligation to realise a work of distortion that conceals it. It comes into play during the day, when the claims of the unconscious desires cannot wait for the individual solution of the dream of the following night. Affective and group ties are then organised, which favour such a fulfilment during waking life.

The analytic situation is particularly favourable to such hysterical identifications in the analysand and analyst alike. They form part of the momentary countertransference of the analyst. It is thus an ordinary mechanism, reversible and useful within analytic sessions, prior to the elaboration of the interpretation.

Freud took up this example of the two women friends who deprived themselves and refused their husbands' offers in 1921 in *Group Psychology and the Analysis of the Ego*. He generalised it to all the affects of loss, disappointment, and lack. Thus, a young girl is disappointed upon receiving a letter from her sweetheart. She feels deep sadness which is transmitted to all the young girls present. They all experience the same heartache, their unconscious Oedipal renunciations.

Freud likened contagiousness with the herd instinct, in the service of the repression of generic Oedipal wishes and of their hallucinatory fulfilment, just after the development in his theory of the drives, which recognised that the traumatic factor is the most elementary quality of all instinctual drives, of life and death. Having attributed the traumatic factor to early seduction, and then to the conflict between the sexual drives and the ego drives, he recognised that every drive is concerned by this traumatic tendency to return to an earlier state, and even to the inorganic and inanimate state.

The notion of lack mentioned earlier proves to have several combined origins: the extinctive tendency inherent to all drives, the stumbling blocks of the psychic work required by this extinctive tendency, and the experience that results from the psychic work inherent to the human condition.

During the elaboration of narcissism and of the conflict between the sexual drives and the desexualised drives, lack was linked to the great vexations of the ego inflicted on human beings, to the disillusionments brought by science obliging man to acknowledge that he is no longer at the centre of the world (Copernic), that he belongs the animal species (Darwin), and that he is not the master of his own house (Freud).

Individual acceptance of such experiences comes up against the temptations to resort to modes of psychic functioning appealing to the group. This conflict is discussed by Freud (1912–1913) in *Totem and Taboo* from its positive angle. The elimination of the requirement of renunciation creates unconscious guilt, which may give rise, through obedience after the event, to a more elaborate group organisation, albeit regressive from the point of view of individual requirements. Psychic modes of functioning that are only expressed through the group have their origin in an exclusion of individual requirements and are thus regressive in comparison with an ideal mode of individual functioning.

So far, I have discussed the influence of Oedipal attractions and of the ambivalence towards the renunciations necessary for maturity which initiate regressions to the infantile register. Thanks to the infantile, the oscillation between night and day responds to these attractions and to this ambivalence. Contagiousness and hysterical identification are daytime responses. When ambivalence towards the work of renunciation dominates, a bond of contagiousness guarantees repression without renunciation. The infantile thus attenuates the traumatic experiences linked to the extinctive tendencies. The register of the infantile recognises the existence of lack and attempts to deny it by means of a theory that makes lack the result of a reduction. For the register of the infantile, there is only one sex.

Certain clinical scenarios teach us that there are no specific childhood contents of traumatic experiences, which prevents the psyche from working on the contents of infantile amnesia. It is here that other potentialities of functioning are brought into play, those that are expressed through the group.

One instance concerns the establishment of narcissism by relying on the narcissism of another person. Hence the propensity to find outside oneself what it is lacking. The outside world is then identified with what can put an end to the experiences of lack. Another contribution of psychoanalysis to group psychology can be seen here, that of narcissistic object relations, relations of complementarity, anaclisis, support, dependence and mutual assistance, and commensality. The genesis of narcissism and its vacillations give rise to the institutions of the city and their functions. They are supposed to compensate for individual experiences of lack and deficiencies by providing from the outside what is lacking within. From the history of narcissism, the reminiscence of an expectation of the outside world is retained. Once again, a certain number of terms refer to the group dimension, those of anaclisis, identification, narcissistic object relations, and commensal relations.

Another instance concerns anti-traumatic solutions seeking to avoid individual traumatic neurosis. The compulsion to repeat observed in the course of sessions linked to the war neuroses taught Freud that there were no childhood contents that made it possible to respond to the traumatic attraction and that there was no narcissistic regression to the maternal womb. Psychic work must be carried out by using the infantile register without being able to use specific childhood contents of traumatic experiences. Infantile sexual theories have their raison d'être here. They create links of causality, accusation, persecution, and conspiracy with external reality. They need to be reinforced by others, hence the promotion of opinion groups.

As soon as Freud recognised that the traumatic dimension is the quality that defines all the drives, he turned towards the collective and the quantitative as a response to this regressive attraction to the point of extinction; traumatic feelings are excluded by an appeal to the masses and to ideologies. Complicity is organised between individuals and the institutions in relation to which they are alienated. The ego ideal is then saturated by ideologies conveyed by a leader to whom charismatic power is attributed. A relationship of shared denial is established between individuals and institutions, between the leader and the people who trust in him. It is no longer a matter of contagiousness, or of anaclisis through complementarity, but of a mass quantitative factor with the aim of eradicating the internal origin of the extinctive tendencies, without hallucinatory wish fulfilment. In general, these are redirected towards an external enemy that must be suppressed or exterminated.

A further instance of potential psychic functioning that can only find expression through the group appeared later on and was not described by Freud. It concerns the actual dimension present in each of us, characterised by the utilisation of tangible reality perceived immediately. The "operational" (*opératoire*) mode of functioning adapts the immediateness of the present environment. The underlying ego ideal is not to escape an internal conflict by creating one on the outside, but to strive for a return to a state of calm, a way of life based on conformism with the surrounding world, a conformism that requires a rupture of the correlations that are established between the external world and instinctual drive life. The conformism of the actual suppresses all sympathetic and erotogenic libidinal excitation between the external world and the instinctual drive sources. The psychic richness of allusions, evocations, metaphors, and poetry is lost. There is no longer any double erotogenic meaning.

Traumatic neurosis appears during sensations of imminent danger. Recourse to the group occurs through alienation to an ideology that externalises the reasons for the traumatic factor. The logic of actual neurosis is different. The ideal refers to a conformism of calm. This solution is sought as soon as restrictions, deprivations, obstacles to carrying out the mourning required by the successive losses inflicted, repeated and sustained humiliations tend to become chronic, without leaving any possible future other than that of ambient conformism.

Sometimes our psychoanalytic institutions are used by our individual potentialities that are in need of a group to manifest and express themselves.

References

Freud, S. (1900). *The interpretation of dreams*. *S.E* (Vol. 4, pp. 147–149).
Freud, S. (1912–1913). *Totem and taboo. SE* (Vol. 13, pp. 1–161).

Chapter 4

Infantile and Institutionalisation

Jasminka Šuljagić

I will firstly try to delineate the realm, work, and modalities of the concept of the infantile and then think about the processes of its institution in mental life, in the outer world, and in the life of social and, particularly, our psychoanalytical institutions.

Positioning the term "infantile" in the last decade of the 19th century, giving it a scenic character (at first in connection with sleeping and dreams: representability, figurability, dramatisation, transposition), and choosing a word to mark its universal presence that extends far beyond its fixed time of childhood, Freud indicated a new era for one concept. He started to discover what would become a new form of discourse, one which would allow for and raise a number of future divergences. Very early, Freud noted the infantile determinants of the "unconscious psychical trace" in "posthumous action" (1896), with "deferred effect" (1898), or in "deferred action" (1897, 1950 [1895]).

Throughout his work and with new discoveries, the infantile gained new outlines and new levels. Many points were included: from dream life, infantile sexuality, towards the questions of narcissism and relations with an object, in relation to principles (pleasure and reality) and processes (primary and secondary); then within the second topography, there were notions about ego ideal and superego, primal repression, regressive tendency to return to earlier states, splitting of the ego, and fetishism. The work and clinical practice of authors after Freud also contribute to this theme.

The infantile is introduced into the psychic life by the process of primal repression (a precursor and necessary condition of repression proper or secondary repression), with the operation of co-excitation, bringing together the soma to body, excitations to drives, and representing drives to the mental field, marking in this way the beginnings of representability and the first amalgamation of drives. Reconstructed retrospectively, it is the first structuralisation of mental life and the first emergence from prehistory. Through primary identification, a "prehistoric unforgettable other person" becomes a "fellow human being", and the psychic landscape started to be differentiated, organised into psychic instances (even Freud expressed reserve towards spacial metaphors, telling us to retain the

DOI: 10.4324/9781032709819-7

coolness of our judgement and not to mistake the scaffolding for the building), and infantile sexuality structured into phases and stages within the organisation of libido.

Made up of many components and passing through a complex course of development, infantile sexuality goes through a "series of developments, combinations, divisions and suppressions, transformation, and rearrangements", but always bearing both sides of its development, testifying about its origin. There is a force with a regressive gravitational attraction, remnants, and reminiscence of the traumatic, even in the model of wish and the fulfilment of a wish, not only in drawing further and further back, "beyond the mnemic images", but also in the very heart of the wish: to repeat and revive, to reinvest and re-establish. On the other hand, there is an opening towards the world of representatives, which, with the help of the first "dissection" (later "splitting"), makes a division into what coincides in a subject with memories of quite similar impressions of their own, of their body, and what is new, non-comparably, a constant structure staying as a thing, with further transposition and animism.

As in *One Thousand and One Nights*, in the very proximity of both extinction and a primal scene, in waiting ("for something which never came", said Freud in 1938), and with projection towards the future in the form of an ideal, the infantile dreams its own dreams, tells its stories, and invents games, along the lines of the diverse streams of its own sexuality of polymorph nature. It is present in narrative, within the setting of sessions, and also in the myths of origins of any institution, traversing from the primeval and prehistoric, led by strong idealisation, mythification of beginnings, and anticipation of the future, accompanied by the urge towards the redirection of this path to less-organised forms, in resistance to what is innovative and changing. From Bion's experience with groups, we know that when any groups of people meet to do a task, there are actually two groups or configurations of mental activity, present at one and the same time: the sophisticated work group, which is "constantly perturbed by influences that come from other group mental phenomena" (Bion, 1961), a group mentality with a culture that causes the individual to regress and to be temporarily caught up in primitive mechanisms and infantile regression. On the other hand, and in another not quite so well-known text, "Psychiatry at a time of crisis" (published in the *British Journal of Medical Psychology* in June 1948), Bion proposed: "It seems that man in his growth cannot solve any problem without immediately opening up more problems which present themselves for their resolution."

We can stop now, briefly, to take a look at what we could call *the historical vignette no 1*.

The increasing foundations of Freud's discoveries bring the need for the constant enlargement of the structure and organisation, starting from the first "congresses", as Freud jokingly called his encounters with Fliess, and the first meetings with Stekel, Adler, Kahane, and Reitler in 1902 (denoting the foundation of the Psychological Wednesday Society, which changed its name to the Vienna Psychoanalytic

Society), all the way to the first real congress in Salzburg, 1908 and the second one in Nuremberg, 1910, with the foundation of the International Psychoanalytic Association (IPA), followed by the establishment of yet one more organisation in 1912 – the Secret Committee.

The first organisational proposals which could be heard at the informal group's Wednesday meeting, according to the minutes of the Vienna Psychoanalytic Society, date from the meeting of 5 February 1908, with the disquietness following the announcement of the first international congress and the formation of a larger international group. It was not accepted at that time, but the establishment of the IPA two years later helped structure the Vienna Psychoanalytic Society and the appointment of Adler as its president. "Until now, the members of the Society have been his guests: now this is no longer feasible. The society must constitute itself and elect a president" (Nunberg & Federn, 1962). A bit later, in 1912, it was the departure of Adler, followed by Stekel, with Jung showing the signs of going the same way, which provided the impetus that led to the formation of the "Secret Committee" consisting of Freud's closest, fully trusted associates. This was the period when Freud was writing *Totem and Taboo* (1913).

With the subtitle *Some Points of Agreement between the Mental Lives of Savages and Neurotics*, as well as later in *Group Psychology and the Analysis of the Ego* (1921) and *The Ego and the Id* (1923), Freud attempted to solve the question of the birth of a social organisation and the fact of institutionalisation and authority. This could be a more serious echo of one his first playful letters to his friend Eduard Silberstein, where Freud noted: "An old superstition has it that no building is sound whose foundations have not cost a human sacrifice" (Boehlich, 1990, cited in Grosskurth, 1991). The problem of institutionalisation or social organisations reappears in its full form in mythical terms. Freud installed the Oedipal complex as "the peak of infantile sexual life", the "nucleus of neurosis", as well as universal fate. Prohibition is posited as the counterpart of repression and cultural renunciation of the work of mourning. Themes of the identification and constitution of authority, with all its harshness and traumatic potential, found their place here.

We can read:

> The clan celebrates the "cruel slaughter of its totem animal and is devouring it raw – blood, flesh and bones."
> Thus it became a duty to repeat the crime of patricide again and again in the sacrifice of the totem animal, whenever, as a result of the changing conditions of life, the cherished fruit of the crime – appropriation of the paternal attributes – threatened to disappear.
> The son's sense of guilt and the son's rebelliousness never become extinct.
>
> (1912)

Institutionalisation is painful, burdened with all previous trends, and what is often emphasised concerning our psychoanalytic institutions is the risk of authoritarianism and dogmatism and the parallel infantilisation of candidates. For them, being in a conflicting transition from analytic relations to belonging to the organisation in the very proximity of transference regression is a very complex question and, surely, not one-sided.

Historical vignette no 2. This is an excerpt from a letter from Sigmund Freud to C. G. Jung from December 22, 1912:

> I regret that my reference to your slip of the pen has irritated you so much, and I feel that your reaction is out of proportion to the occasion. Your reproach that I abuse psychoanalysis for the purpose of keeping my pupils in infantile dependency and that therefore I myself am responsible for their "infantile" behavior toward me, as well as everything else that you base on this assumption, I won't judge, because all judgment concerning oneself is so difficult and doesn't carry conviction. I will just furnish you with some factual material for the basis of your theory and leave it to you to revise it. In Vienna, for instance, I am accustomed to hearing the opposite reproach.
>
> (Freud, 1912a).

In the same day, Freud also wrote to Ferenzci, explaining:

> As prior history I note that he wrote recently that he had the intention of writing a critique of Adler. I responded it would be good, because in Vienna word is stubbornly being spread around that he was once again swinging over to Adler. Whereupon he said: "Even Adler's cronies don't regard me as one of *yours*." Then I asked him if he was objective enough to consider this slip without anger, and now, thereupon, his letter.
>
> My reaction to this is difficult. He is obviously disposed to provoke me so that the responsibility for the break will fall to me and he can say that I can't tolerate analysis. On the other hand, if I respond calmly and moderately and treat him like one of our patients when he gets into a fit of cursing, he will think I am afraid and will get more audacious; or I can continue to treat him, undaunted. In such an awkward situation I will postpone reacting, especially until our journal is secure, and I will send the namby-pamby [lammherzig] draft of my reply to you instead of to him.
>
> (Freud, 1912b)

According to the careful analysis by Émile Benveniste (2016), the notion of "authority" (derived from *auctor)* is the agent noun from *augeo*, which is usually translated as "grow, increase". "To increase", as is suggested, is a secondary and weakened sense of *augeo*, where in its oldest uses it denoted not the increase in something which already exists but the act of producing from within itself, a creative act which causes something to arise, even divine in principle, used in retracing the genesis in the universal rhythm of birth and death. Every word pronounced with authority determines a change in the world; it creates something, and the notion expressed by *auctor* is diversified according to the different contexts in which it is used, but they all go clearly back to the primary sense "cause to appear, promote". Or to sum up: "This authority – *auctoritas* – with which a man must be invested for his utterances to have the force of law is not, as is often stated, the power of promoting growth (*augere*), but the force of 'causing to exist.'" Maybe in a similar manner, "to care for" is one notion, and "to govern" is another. In Indo-European vocabulary, "to reflect", "to measure", "to govern", and "to care for" are distinct concepts which can neither coexist in the same forms nor be derived from one another.

This difference, necessary for the life of institutions, is rightly what remains beyond the realm of the infantile. We can leave aside the question of whether it is also a sign of the world we live in, where "[t]here is no such thing as authority" (Foucault, 1980), "we are no longer in a position to know what authority really is" (Arendt, 1961), and "the actual essence of this phenomenon has rarely attracted any attention" (Kojeve, 2014) but investigate it slightly closer in regard to our theme, approaching the end of this presentation.

The structure of the differentiation between "grow, increase" and "cause to appear, create" and its ignorance presents the germ and the last bastion of the culture of the infantile. From its genesis, it is inclined to overcome all that is lacking; in its later stage, it came to proclaim that differences arose only from growth, in line with "what is missing, will grow". This is a touching testimony of disavowal of differences between the sexes and, by this, of the genitality as well and, more than that, of an unbearable and unpresentable absence from the primal scene as the place of the origin.

In the attempt of equalisation, we are then returning towards "totemic community of brothers", group mentality streaming toward uniformity, where a group is not organised around the leader but around the group itself, a group which is self-generated, as well as to the now more widespread insistence on variation and differences, but without recognising crucial differentiations and the truth of creating – "they must all renounce their father's heritage", and "battles begin afresh" (Freud, 1921).

Finally, I would like us to remember to whom amongst sons/brothers in the "scientific myth of the father of the primal horde" Freud (in 1921) assigned the task of freeing himself from the group and taking over the father's role, what preceded that, and how it reflects on our theme. He was, as is suggested, an individual in the exigency of his longing, the first epic poet after acknowledging the mother deities. The advance was achieved in his imagination, and he invented the heroic myth – as the father had been the boy's first ideal, so "in the hero who aspires to the father's place the poet now created the first ego ideal" (ibid.). The infantile is reinstated and transformed, through this act finding its paths towards both reality and imagination.

References

Arendt, H. (1961). What is authority? In *Between past and future* (pp. 91–141). The Viking Press.
Benveniste, E. (2016). *Dictionary of Indo-European concepts and society*. Hau Books.
Bion, W. (1948). Psychiatry at a time of crisis. *British Journal of Medical Psychology*, XXI(2), 81–89.
Bion, W. R. (1961). *Experiences in groups and other papers*. Tavistock Publication.
Foucault, M. (1980). *Power/Knowledge: Selected interviews and other writings 1972–1977*. Google Books: Colin Gordon.
Freud, S. (1896). *Heredity and the aetiology of the neuroses. SE* (Vol. 3, pp. 141–156).
Freud, S. (1897). *Letter 75 extracts from the Fliess papers. SE* (Vol. 1, pp. 268–271).
Freud, S. (1898). *Sexuality in the aetiology of the neuroses. SE* (Vol. 3, pp. 259–285).
Freud, S. (1912a). Letter from Sigmund Freud to C. G. Jung, December 22, 1912. In *Letters of Sigmund Freud 1873–1939* (Vol. 51, pp. 295–296).
Freud, S. (1912b). Letter from Sigmund Freud to Sándor Ferenczi, December 22, 1912. In *The Correspondence of Sigmund Freud and Sándor Ferenczi, Volume 1, 1908–1914* (Vol. 25, pp. 445–447).
Freud, S. (1913). *Totem and taboo: Some points of agreement between the mental lives of savages and neurotics (1913 [1912–13]). SE* (Vol. 13, pp. 7–162).
Freud, S. (1921). *Group psychology and the analysis of the ego. SE* (Vol. 18, pp. 65–144).
Freud, S. (1923). *The ego and the Id. SE* (Vol. 19, pp. 1–66).
Freud, S. (1938). *Findings, ideas, problems. SE* (Vol. 23, pp. 299–300).
Freud, S. (1950). *Project for a scientific psychology (1950 [1895]). SE* (Vol. 1, pp. 281–391).
Grosskurth, P. (1991). *The secret ring: Freud's inner circle and the politics of psychoanalysis*. Addison-Wesley.
Kojeve, A. (2014). *The notion of authority*. Verso.
Nunberg, H., & Federn, E. (1962). *Minutes of the Vienna psychoanalytic society (1906–1908)* (Vol. 1). International University Press.

The Familiar and the Unfamiliar in Psychoanalytic Institutions

About Stumbling Across Otherness

Chapter 5

Interweavings

Unconscious Singularity, Group Mentality, and Reconstructed History

Bernard Chervet

The aim of our ad hoc group is to study and to think about institutional matters in psychoanalytic organisations.

Firstly, I would like to say a few words about our method of working, and about a fundamental conflict between two wishes: being different from others and being like others. Actually, this conflict concerns all identifications that take place within all groups, and therefore within our organisations, and which make it possible both to reduce the gap of otherness between group members and to recognise this otherness, to keep the other and to leave him. This is the issue of separation, loss, and mourning.

Gradually, we discovered that we were referring to material from several origins, and we soon noticed that there were three levels of thinking that needed to be distinguished if we wanted to avoid confusion and also to avoid participating in the tendency of group psychology to interpret and reduce the matters we want to study solely from the angle of the pleasure principle, that is, avoiding and projecting outside what is foreign in order to support what is familiar as our identity.

If our method seeks to be attentive to differences, we also have to recognise that these three levels are always interwoven, hence the complexity.

First origin. The material of the sessions; the free associations of patients who are members or candidates of one of the analytical organisations; each of us, of course!

Second origin. The discourses (the official ones and the others) which are made within the organisations on all matters: conflicts, crises, issues, and splits which happen or have happened in them. This is the aim of the interviews.

Third origin. The historical studies made by analysts or non-analysts about the history of some analytical organisations, and about psychoanalysis in a country.

Fourth origin. Our theoretical background, which is involved in our listening of all the material we gather.

These four origins involve three different levels of thinking.

The *first* is the regressive free association of the sessions. It has to be heard through the specific analytic way of listening, evenly suspended attention, and to be interpreted in the light of individual material, such as reminiscences, and as deferred effects of traumatic infantile life, with primal fantasies, unconscious Oedipal

DOI: 10.4324/9781032709819-9

wishes, the claims of infantile sexuality and the narcissistic identifications, the regressive attraction of drives, and so on. This allows us to listen to the links between the current issues and the past ones, and to listen to the transference of the unconscious wishes which are involved in the analogy between both.

Personal psychic work makes use of the events in daily life to give concrete reality to, and to actualise, the means which were used during childhood. The traumatic dimension can be recognised as well as the processes which are used by doing specific psychic work on it, such as hate or unconscious identifications with some ideology, or denial.

The *second* are the discourses that the collective psychology produces in the groups to try to deal with the traumatic events which happen within it, to give itself explanations for conflicts, crisis, splits, and any other issues. The means which are used are not the same. Some aspects are emphasised, amplified, idealised; others are put aside, put into latency, forgotten, excluded, and denied; while others are invented, transformed, cancelled, concealed by censorship and repression, which produce distortion and shared denial. In the best of cases, there are several explanations, thus several stories, histories with several interpretations, contradicting each other, and commanding varying degrees of conviction. These discourses can be interpreted as attempts to put a part of the truth outside, to distance lack and absence from one's feelings. They are "après-coups" (Nachträglichkeit; *deferred effects*) produced by the group mentality.

The *third* is the construction of history, with the use of documents and other sources of information arising from an investigation of materials in a wide range of fields.

This way is an attempt to approach the historical truth, which is very different from individual truth, and from the "truth" of the group. These reconstructions have to accept doubts and lack, and to abandon conviction. They attempt to give interpretations of the events by taking into account the first and the second level, but they stay outside. They use the models of the first and second levels, which allowed their specific interpretations, but they do not seek to have access to the unconscious meanings. These reconstructions can be very relevant and very plausible from the point of view of truth and yet be false.

Now it becomes clear that an important point of our understanding of our topic is the relationships in groups to difference and lack.

Chapter 6

Differentiations and Their Reversals

Jasminka Šuljagić

Thinking about the familiar/unfamiliar draws our attention towards difference, the me/not me differentiation, and all other differences, considered by our psychoanalytic theories as constitutive. We are, in our very essence, already and always constituted by what is outside of us, regardless of whether conceived as the "prehistoric, unforgettable other person", "Nebenmensch", "containment and reverie", or "environment mother". Moreover, it could be said that we are also constituted by differences which are repudiated, by our very endeavours to refuse and reduce them to the logic of the same.

We can follow here the path which led from the "first mental activity" (Freud, 1900), whose aim is to produce perceptual identity, by way of the negation and the language of oral impulses (devour – spit it out), to the disavowal of a perception of differences. Alongside, there are "roundabout paths" which recognise difference and alienation but include psychic work, both that of mourning and the anticipation of new units, more differentiated in themselves and in relation to the environment.

Belonging to groups revives these confliction dualities, placing them at its very center.

"We do not know why such sensitiveness should have been directed to just these details of differentiation", Freud tells us in *Group Psychology and the Analysis of the Ego*, speaking first of aversions and intolerance towards strangers, especially when they come together in larger units. The source of such readiness for hatred is, he says, unknown, and he ascribes an elementary character to it, referring to the then recently described polarity of love and hatred with a hypothetical opposition between life and death drives. Then follows the known description of a reversal of what was first a hostile feeling into a common affectionate tie with a person who is put in the place of the ego ideal, which consequently leads to mutual identification. What has already been a kind of individual alienation (with traces of all previous ones) – the forming of the ego ideal as a double, with multiple foreign distances – becomes connective tissue for new affective ties; the members of the group are united in their strangeness. We should not forget the mythical killing of the primeval father, whereby the brothers, all equals, become united in

DOI: 10.4324/9781032709819-10

a joint denial of both the murderous act and the loss, celebrating the appropriation of father's attributes in totem feasts. But they cannot use what caused the murder to occur, and none of them ever becomes the father who was removed. Our identifications, among them the first and most important one with the father in our own "personal prehistory" ("perhaps it would be safer to say 'with the parents'", added Freud, 1923), are marked by attempts to keep the other, and to separate and differentiate from him – group relations might be used to escape this conflict.

This twofold potential in the forming of a group, greater differentiation in forming new units and the lessening of individual distinctiveness, is expressed in Bion's description of the parallel existence of two configurations of mental activity, present at one and the same time, when any group of people meets to do something – two pictures or, in actuality, two groups. We know of this distinction between a work group, "constantly perturbed by influences that come from other group mental phenomena" (Bion, 1961), called the basic assumptions group. To three basic assumptions groups (dependency, fight/flight, and pairing), all invariably underlain by a group mentality of uniformity, Turquet added a fourth, which was a basic assumption of oneness, while Lawrence proposed the basic assumption group emphasising separateness, which hates the idea of "we", as the opposite (Lawrence et al., 1996).

Before taking a look at the life of our psychoanalytical organisations, it is worth returning once more to the very notion of "differentiation and its details". What had been implied in his earlier works, Freud explicitly stated in 1921: "Each of the mental differentiations that we have become acquainted with represents a fresh aggravation of the difficulties of mental functioning, increases its instability, and may become the starting-point for its breakdown, that is, for the onset of a disease." He goes on to say that by being born, we have taken a step towards the perception of a changing external world and the beginnings of the discovery of objects; with this is associated the fact that we cannot endure the new state of things for long, and we periodically revert from it, in our sleep, to our former condition of absence of stimulation and avoidance of objects.

With this short conceptual sketch, we could think about the mechanisms of such periodical reversion within our psychoanalytical organisations, having in mind the obstacles in their formation, the hardships in taking new, organisational steps and changes, and coping with diversity altogether.

Miniatures

A) In 1947, the Dutch Society, "in an urgent longing for international contact", organised a conference of European psychoanalysts in Amsterdam, from 24 to 26 May, states Han Groen-Prakken in the text "A European Organisation for Psychoanalysis – Why, How and When?" There were more than 100 participants from 11 European countries, but although the conference was an obvious success, 11 years passed before a second attempt at a European reunion was made. Also, there were many meetings and discussions before the establishment of the European Psycho-Analytical Federation, the founding period extended over nearly three years, from 1966 to 1969.

A partial explanation for the difficult start to the Federation in the 1960s might well be a reluctance on the part of several European Societies to give up their state of "splendid isolation". . . . Every Society in every country still has its own cultural and linguistic background, and each separate country has been at war with every other separate country at some time in the last few hundred years. A basic sense that "we are different" and a mild basic mistrust will probably persist in Europe for ever. A contrary affective impulse, which is apparently stronger than the dividing one, is the fact that psychoanalysts need each other.

(Groen-Prakken, 1986)

Developments were similar in Freud's time, with the forming of the IPA and the congresses at Salzburg, Nüremberg, and Weimar, with the Vienna Society formed from the Psychological Wednesday Society, and in the history of the beginnings of all individual societies.

B) Once founded, we find ourselves in a multitude of various relations towards that which is outside and more or less strange and alien. This raises the issue of membership – who is suitable to be a member of a psychoanalytical society (on 20 February 1919, Ernst Jones, without any rules on how to restrict membership, dissolved the London Psycho-Analytical Society and founded the British Psycho-Analytical Society (King, 1979). Or it could be a matter of professional recognition by the community, the healthcare system, for instance (28 meetings with the committee of the British Medical Association in the early days of the same society – a topic so troublesome for many societies nowadays). Then there is the question of lay candidates and the relationship of every society with other professional groups (e.g. with the Tavistock clinic in the 1940s in the current illustration). The aforementioned society, on a "peaceful compromising island" (as Strachey, in the early spring of 1940 and down with a feverish cold, wrote to Edward Glower, Chairman of the Training Committee (King & Steiner, 1991), accepted and assimilated foreign colleagues in large numbers, while simultaneously faced with a dispersal of the society's own members, owing to the attack on London. Besides, what are the circumstances of every society when theoretical divergences become too apparent and insurmountable, or the discord among the members so pronounced, that a rift seems inevitable?

C) Freud refers to the unity of members of a group through the ego ideal embodied in the leader, which enables mutual identification and modification of hostile feelings.

Can, indeed, those in charge of our institutions be situated at that place, in terms of pursued values and objectives, in a prevalent group culture of pairs and dyads formed with one's own analyst and supervisor? "If a conflict should arise, who am I to be loyal to, to the president or to my analyst?" are the words of the nominee for general secretary of the society, anticipating a conflict and the issue of loyalty.

D) Challenges of alterity, with its transference remnants, strongly impact the attitude of members toward their own organisations. Repudiation and denial of otherness from personal analysis find a place in the institutions themselves, consequently seen as alien and so becoming places which belong to someone else. One of the rare ways by which our organisations cease to be so unfamiliar to members is in their persistent craving for a family model and their endless use of family metaphors, with focus on the internal life of the group, rather than on work and tasks. In that family, if not a tribal organisation, the very idea of organisation and organisational roles is profoundly estranged, if not downright repulsive. With a uniform group mentality and sometimes blurred differentiation between the ego and the ego ideal, our institutions have a tendency to oscillate between "we" equality and "me" apartness, in many respects narrowing the scope for group work, both in terms of their inner space and in relation to the external reality of the environment.

E) Once, psychoanalysis was in the position of a (critical) reflection of what was exterior to it, the times and the world in which it was emerging, deeply changing the climate of those times and that world. What is its position today? What is it that we now have to say about events which worried humankind, about our post-truth era?

Trembling over its own survival, "our science" is waiting for approval for its existence from the outside, for some crucial proof and confirmation, be it by neuroscience, the healthcare system, or public opinion. Instead of dialogue and differentiated thinking, we often try to adapt ourselves, and slightly disguised, to seduce others, in collusion with their values.

To whom are we addressing our words today? Where are our listeners?

References

Bion, W. R. (1961). *Experiences in groups*. Tavistock Publications.
Freud, S. (1900). *The interpretation of dreams*. SE (Vol. 4, pp. 9–627).
Freud, S. (1921). *Group psychology and the analysis of the ego*. SE (Vol. 18, pp. 65–144).
Freud, S. (1923). *The ego and the Id*. SE (Vol. 19, pp. 1–66).
Groen-Prakken, H. (1986). A European organization for psychoanalysis – why, how and when?. *Psychoanalysis in Europe, EPF Bulletin, 26*, 11–68.
King, P. (1979). The contributions of Ernest Jones to the British psycho-analytical society. *International Journal of Psycho-Analysis, 60*, 280–284.
King, P., & Steiner, R. (1991). *The Freud-Klein controversies 1941–45. New Library of Psychoanalysis* (Vol. 11, pp. 1–942). Tavistock Publications & Routledge.
Lawrence, G., Bain A., & Gould, L. (1996). The fifth basic assumption. *Free Associations, 6* Part 1 (37), 2855.

Chapter 7

On the Defensive Use of Psychoanalytical Concepts

Franziska Ylander

In this chapter, I would like to discuss the fate of some consequences of how we may use, and misuse, psychoanalytical concepts – concepts that we, as analysts, are fundamentally identified with. Many of these concepts are nowadays also seamlessly integrated in media language and in cultural texts and narratives. In other words, they are part of a common language shared by each and every one in many different contexts. Thereby, they are also an unconsciously integrated part of our language and of our minds – relatively independent of psychoanalytical theory and psychoanalytic practice.

In relation to psychoanalysis, or rather psychoanalysts, I am using the concept of "identification" to pinpoint a specific and sought-for experience of being an analyst. This experience could be expressed in something like: "These concepts are familiar to me as I am a psychoanalyst." For psychoanalysts, psychoanalytical concepts are part of a familiar and shared language, created for and used to understand the inner world of the individual analysand.

All psychoanalysts probably enter the training and, in fact, most important, their personal analysis with an idealising transference to psychoanalysis. This includes private hopes of inner freedom and self-knowledge. During this long journey of development and exploration, we have also all consequently been confronted with the unavoidable disappointment of losing omnipotence and control. It is important to highlight the ambiguity and never-ending struggle for freedom from "the limits of reality" – basically an effort to restore omnipotence. This can lead to different kinds of developments – one way would be to "try to get a grip on their personal problems and solve these as much as possible through psychoanalysis" (Vlietstra, 2015), and another way is to focus "on getting control of their Self and their environment, and find in psychoanalysis a tool to realize this". A happy cooperation between these two tracks, these two capacities, is what one would wish for in our work with patients – not just either-or, "empathic-relational opposed to technical-instrumental, emotional-romantic against rational-rule orientated" (Vlietstra, 2015).

Somewhat simplified, one can say that huge parts of our mental life contain elements presenting themselves as seemingly contradictory and ambiguous. Sometimes the theoretical psychoanalytical concepts referring to such elements are also

DOI: 10.4324/9781032709819-11

particularly suitable to express ambiguity and distrust when displaced from its intended task of denominating a trait of the inner world.

I find this very close to what Robert Waelder – an old favourite of mine – presented in his 1936 paper "The Principle of Multiple Functioning". Waelder writes, "Psychoanalysis . . . perceives man's being both impulsively driven, and his being purposely directed" (Waelder, 1936).

And further: "No attempted solution of a problem is possible which is not of such a type that it does not at the same time, in some way or other represent an attempted solution of *other* problems." For better or for worse, psychoanalytical concepts can be, and often are, applied in other settings than those intended for the understanding and exploration of the world of the individual. Not surprisingly, this can happen in contexts involving groups, organisations, and institutional systems. One may ask oneself: Is there a risk that we alienate ourselves from important psychoanalytical concepts by misusing our "common language" in a diluted and defensive way? Or is it perhaps more interesting to explore to what extent our identity as psychoanalysts and our joint identification with a psychoanalytical "language" of concepts contributes to the character of conflicts within and between our institutions, and the scenarios of drama on our institutional battlefields.

How, then, might the principle of multiple functioning manifest itself in psychoanalytical organisations?

As I have already pointed out, identification with crucial aspects of psychoanalytic thinking and theoretical concepts is fundamental in becoming an analyst. This implies feelings of recognition and familiarity, professional self-esteem, and trust. But likewise, if we keep the principle of multiple functioning in mind, identification and internalisation of basic psychoanalytical concepts also tend to work as a place for retreat and defence, and useful as expressions of our everlasting ambiguity and resistance.

On an individual level, at one point or another, there is probably always a competition between the two tracks *insight and/or control*, not always in opposition, but certainly different. One or the other might finally dominate the development of one's identity as psychoanalyst. As already said, one way to go is to aim for self-knowledge and personal development; another track will treasure the task to gain and systematise knowledge, not least theoretically. The inner need to know oneself will always be accompanied by an unescapable unconscious wish to restore early omnipotence and the illusion of control. This aspect of the everlasting influence of what we call the unconscious has doomed us all to run the risk of displacing our psychoanalytical concepts in defensive manoeuvres, irrespective of which track has come to dominate in the development of one's psychoanalytic identity.

As I just said, these two tracks are certainly part of us all, sometimes struggling, sometimes cooperating. Of particular interest for our discussion of institutional matters is how they manifest themselves in polarised situations, like crisis situations within our psychoanalytic institutions. The temptation to project the rejected and disowned parts into others is always hard to escape in all kinds of conflicts – not least within institutions.

> One can reflect on our common difficulties to stand differences – i.e., differences in power, in competence, as well as in positions and status. Splitting and projecting are mechanisms often involved in the effort to avoid difference. It is an easily available and common way to handle many situations of Impending chaos, and power struggle – not least in our psychoanalytical organisations.
>
> (Vlietstra, 2015)

Another, rather striking way of managing differences and provocations are efforts to "familiarise" what is perceived as alien or threatening. By "interpreting," which is rather a "pseudo-interpreting", by using a familiar psychoanalytic concept, one risks to unwittingly label, and thereby probably try to disarm and control, disturbing statements of "others." This way, by "familiarising", one is using the insights of psychoanalytical exploration as a "diagnostic" tool and simultaneously avoiding the ongoing exploration of one's personal ongoing internal power struggles.

Listening to spoken opinions like, "This guy is such a narcissist . . ." or "Well, she's a really hysteroid person . . ." in social settings and group exchanges, is probably quite well known to us all.

It is interesting to note this closeness to diagnostic thinking; the temptation to use insight and knowledge in an attempt to control anxiety, helplessness, or feelings of inferiority is familiar.

An important aspect of "identification" is idealisation, that is, the psychoanalyst's idealisation of psychoanalysis and our institutions. Idealisation cannot exist without its counterpart, denigration, and even patricide (Orduz, 2015). We may start our training analysis embedded in hope for achieving an idealised conception of psychoanalysis, which could free us from the limitations of reality. The unavoidable disillusionment and the limitations of this aspect of the psychoanalytic endeavour can, by extension, lead to break-ups and splits – when appearing or acted out within institutions.

Psychoanalytic organisations are, and will always be, imprinted with this oscillation between idealisation and crisis, between the defending of dogmas and the fight to annihilate them. Psychoanalysis and what belongs to psychoanalysts will always encounter conflicts adhering in a probably specific way to our kind of institutions. This implies that psychoanalysis will always tend to question its implicit "institutionality", not least on matters representing limitations and control.

Let me repeat again: there are at least two sets of concepts, one for individuals, one for groups. With the multiple-function principle in mind, we must not forget the – perhaps unavoidable – risk of using the psychoanalytic language created for the inner world as a defensive tool to circumvent the restraints and anxieties of a more complex and manifold reality. In situations characterised by conflict and crisis, our individual minds are prey to idealisation and its counterpart, denigration – as well as to projection of unwished-for parts of oneself.

During the early 2020s, we have all been confronted with serious external threats to institutions (pandemic, political crisis), as well as with the reality of physical downfall or survival of the individual (wartime, economic survival). Among many extremely serious and complicated reactions, there has also appeared a tendency to authoritarian tendencies within psychoanalytical institutions, and a kind of "non-thinking" yes/no, either/or attitude. Within psychoanalytic organisations, huge parts of internal crises are connected to issues on transmission of power, very often appearing in connection to matters of oversight and training. This kind of crisis events usually include matters of authority and responsibility, and of the impact of experience and evaluation of competence. Questions of power and of who is in charge – who has authority – are certainly crucial on many levels and contexts in all organisations. In psychoanalytic societies, they are often acted out within the training functions.

The problem area of responsibility and competence certainly has an impact on other extremely important areas in the organisations, such as hesitance and cautiousness in relation to taking positions. To be invited to take on or aspire to take on responsibility and leadership is strikingly often evaded in psychoanalytical societies.

Psychoanalytic interpretations of unconscious motives of the individual analyst are not helpful in understanding a Zeitgeist; even if a threat of patricide might be in the air, principles of group dynamics are more appropriate on an institutional level. On the other hand, psychoanalytical concepts are extremely useful as instrument for clarifying complicated dynamics in the wake of institutional crises, not least in hindsight, and thereby useful for a more generalised understanding of future problems.

Changes like splitting or fusion certainly, in themselves, contain all the components of a potential crisis. A clear formulation of the institutional level of the task is of vast importance to those preparing the ground for such a fundamental decision and change. To inform the membership and communicate as much and as transparently as possible is of utmost necessity. It is just as important to realise that independent of how much you share and how high a degree of transparency you achieve, there will always be individuals in the membership who have never been informed.

I want to emphasise that candidates are always the losers when conflicts progress into standstills or, even worse, run amok into break-ups and splits. Candidates tend to be regarded as children and, in crises, unfortunately often unwittingly treated in abusive ways. My idea is that this is a defensive misuse of the concept of transference – "Not in front of the children!" What is warded off is the fact that – independent of the status of candidates in the specific psychoanalytic society – candidates are a dependent but integrated part of our psychoanalytical institutions and must be treated according to this reality "in their own right".

Finally, the successful working through of a major change or a crisis does not protect any society from new challenges on all kind of levels, not least the defensive misuse of psychoanalytical concepts in efforts to ward off painful closeness to threats of loss and chaos. At the same time, the well-integrated understanding of the dynamics of psychoanalysis, not least via its concepts, is an indispensable tool when you try to navigate through any crise in your psychoanalytic organisation.

References

Orduz, F. (2015). Institutional break-ups. Panel *Societies in transition*, 49th IPA Congress 2015.

Vlietstra, D. (2015). Splitting of psychoanalytical societies, some thoughts on the dynamics. Panel *Societies in transition*, 49th IPA Congress 2015.

Waelder, D. (1930). The principle of multiple functioning. Observations on over-determination. *The Psychoanalytic Quarterly*, 5(1), 45–62. (Original work published 1936)

Part IV

Paths and Figures of Intimacy Within Psychoanalytic Rooms and Organisations

Chapter 8

Fervour, Traces, and Figures of Intimacy

Jasminka Šuljagić

I will start with something slightly remote from this theme but still connected with it, both as an introduction and also as a way to express our gratitude to our host city. This is about a book from 1923, titled *Fervor de Buenos Aires*, written by 23-year-old Jorge Luis Borges at the time of his brief return to Argentina, after having spent several years in Europe. These 46 poems are devoted to the town of his childhood, found again upon his returning, reconstructed, to his surprise and shock. The book was printed in a rush, in five days. He said that no proofreading was done, no table of contents was provided, and the pages were unnumbered. His sister made a woodcut for the cover, and 300 copies were printed, most of which he just gave away. J. L. Borges asked the editor of one of the oldest and most renowned literary journals of that time to put copies into the pockets of the coats that Argentine writers had hung on the hallway coat hooks.

In 1925, just two years after this adventure, the author wrote that he realised that poetry, for which he thought to be flying freely and carelessly, started drawing a geometrical figure in the air of time. He added that it is a beautiful and sad surprise to hear that the former act, so natural and free, is nothing more than the beginning of a ritual (Borges, 1970).

In our thinking about intimacy, we can follow this twofold movement, finding again in reality what belongs to reminiscences, from the fervour of an encounter to figures of the already known and repeating. The space of these transformations is an intimate space, and the poetics of its vicissitudes alongside the attempts to avoid them can be traced on individual levels, as well as in the life of the dyad, the group, and the organisation.

We are familiar with the following photo. It shows one of the first IPA congresses, the third one, the Weimar Congress, held in September 1911. The total attendance was 55, including some visitors, which was slightly over half the total membership of the international association, established shortly before that.

Although the history of the institutionalisation of psychoanalysis was, at that moment, at its very beginning and this group might now seem idyllic to us, many temptations, together with ways of overcoming them, have already arisen. "They have learned to tolerate a piece of reality", Freud replied quietly when James

DOI: 10.4324/9781032709819-13

Figure 8.1 International Psychoanalytic Congress, 1911. Sigmund Freud and Carl Jung seen at the centre of the group.

Source: World History Archive/Alamy Stock Photo.

Putnam, a congress attendant from America, congratulated him on the quality of his followers.

The growing foundations of Freud's discoveries bring a need for the constant enlargement of the structure and organisation: from the first "congresses", as Freud jokingly called his encounters with Fliess, and the first meetings with Stekel, Adler, Kahane, and Reitler in 1902 (denoting the foundation of the Psychological Wednesday Society, which changed its name to the Vienna Psychoanalytic Society), all the way to the first real congress in Salzburg, 1908 and the second one in Nuremberg, 1910, with the foundation of the International Psychoanalytic Association, followed by the establishment of yet one more organisation in 1912 – the Secret Committee. This was the period when Freud was writing *Totem and Taboo*, preparing his work, reading a large amount of literature on the subject in 1910, formulating the title by August 1911, and successively finishing four essays, in 1912 and 1913.

All these foundational acts, which unfolded in parallel with writing about them as belonging to the mythical past, were renewed attempts at finding a form, or we could say "a frame" (in both of its meanings: Bleger, 2013), for initial fervour, and for hate, rivalry, and violence, always present.

The first congress in Salzburg, in 1908, which we heard was merely a "private meeting" with the name "First Congress for Freudian Psychology" and lasted for only one day, had "no Chairman, no Secretary, no Treasurer, no Council, no kind of Sub-Committee whatsoever, and", as Jones said, "best of all – no Business Meeting!" However, it included a five-hour-long presentation of the case of the Rat Man:

> He [Freud] sat at the end of a long table along the sides of which we were gathered and spoke in his usual low but distinct conversational tone. He began at the Continental hour of eight in the morning and we listened with rapt attention. At eleven he broke off, suggesting we had had enough. But we were so absorbed that we insisted on his continuing, which he did until nearly one o'clock.
>
> (Jones, 1955)

The main theme of this case presentation, as we know, concerned a conjunction of love and hate, a struggle between two forces, which in *Totem and Taboo* Freud also said lies at the root of many important cultural institutions (Freud, 1913). Paths of intimacy in groups always lean on the enactment of these paradigmatic dualities, either in the form of the mythical killing of the primeval father or in the finding of a prototype for the festive joint ego ideal, always in an attempt to deny the complexity of mutual bonds. In the establishment of systems of identifications, recognizable lines must be maintained, including the (re)constitution of the frame as one of the first and most important. An institution itself, as a frame, could serve as a "depository of the undifferentiated and non-dissolved portion of the primitive symbiotic links" (Bleger, 1967) or as a defence against them (Jaques, 1955).[1] It exists as a dumb presence, mainstay, or bulwark, which reveals itself when it breaks, blocks, or is on the verge of rupture.

In these formative years, the establishment of one organisational frame makes visible the threat of losing the previous, more intimate one. In other words, it makes obvious the complacent forgetfulness of its presence, with an immediate urge for tougher rules (rituals) which would fix and conserve it, or which would form a new frame as a new institution.

In 1908, members of the Vienna Psychological Wednesday Society, in great distress after the announcement of the international congress and the formation of a larger international group, suddenly recognised with surprise that they were not the professor's guests anymore but, of necessity, had to become an organisation. The threat of losing their special closeness to Freud within their familiar circle led to the constitution of the Vienna Psychoanalytic Society, but only after much turmoil and many attempts to impose strict rules, and to abolish "intellectual communism", as they called it.

Similar things happened during the constitution of the IPA, with Ferenczi's assertion of the necessity for all papers delivered by any psychoanalyst to be first submitted for approval to the president of the association. This was not accepted at that time, but one definite obligation undertaken by the members of the newly formed organisation was not to make any public departure from the fundamental tenets of psychoanalytic theory before discussing those views with the others. This was the "Secret Committee", Freud's inner circle of ring-wearers, a small group of trustworthy analysts forming a sort of Old Guard around him (positioned separately from the IPA). After many upheavals, this Secret Committee ceased to exist in 1927, its members assuming the place of IPA officers.

We live those pieces of reality, at various axes and perspectives, in our own societies, looking for its shapes with fervour, to be situated in them and to overcome them. Our Institutional Matters Group attempts to learn from this and to use it for reflection and study.

Note

1 E. Jaques (1955) said that social institutions are unconsciously used as a defence against psychotic anxiety; J. Bleger (1967) believed them to be the depository of the psychotic part of the personality, that is, the undifferentiated and non-dissolved portion of the primitive symbiotic links.

References

Bleger, J. (1967). Psychoanalysis of the psychoanalytic frame. *International Journal of Psycho-Analysis*, *48*, 511–519.

Bleger, J. (2013). *Symbiosis and ambiguity: A psychoanalytic study*. Routledge.

Borges, J. L. (1970, September 19). Autobiographical notes. *The New Yorker*.

Freud, S. (1913). *Totem and taboo: Some points of agreement between the mental lives of savages and neurotics (1913 [1912–13])*. *SE* (Vol. 13, pp. 7–162).

Jaques, E. (1955). Social systems as a defence against persecutory and depressive anxiety. In Heimann, P., Klein, M., Money-Kyrle, R.E., & Trust, M.K. (Eds.), *New directions in psycho-analysis*. Tavistock Publications.

Jones, E. (1955). *Sigmund Freud life and work, Volume two: Years of maturity 1901–1919* (pp. 1–507). The Hogarth Press.

Chapter 9

When Institutional Disorders Occur Instead of the Psychic Activities of Private Intimacy

Bernard Chervet

The theme intimacy immediately evokes the very private atmosphere of our psychoanalytic consultation rooms. Even if the term *intimacy* is not part of the psychoanalytic corpus, it spontaneously enters into association with the analytic situation, with the proximity between two individuals, both physical and confidential, and with the singular gathering up of the transference which combines pervasive and significant current issues with a misunderstanding about the nature of the demand. The transference is sustained by the fundamental rule, as expressed by Freud (1940): "complete candour on one side, strict discretion on the other." This rule exploits a first and enigmatic tendency without which no therapeutic approach to the psyche could take place, namely, the propensity for unconscious psychic processes to be transposed onto the psyche of an "other", in order to gain access to their efficiency, an "other" whom Freud calls the *Nebenmensch, the fellow human being* (the close human being). Of course, the processes set up in the past with the characters from childhood will tend to repeat themselves and resist any sort of evolution. This is the most commonly recognised meaning of the term *transference* as resistance. This fellow human being, a supportive figure for the infant's future development, is attributed with an authority of mental functioning. This transfer of authority is indispensable for psychic growth, both in childhood and in analysis. This "other" facilitates identification with his own psychic processes. It is felt that he is able to provide satisfactions, to accept the role of hate involved in separating from others, and also able to tolerate the transfer of authority, that is, to help the child identify with an accomplished mode of mental functioning. To achieve this effect of the growth of psychic processes, the method of the fundamental rule, free association, and elaboration through interpretation promotes the development of all kinds of *regressive and passive psychic work*, such as the dreamwork, the session talk, the paths of auto-erotism and fantasy, the sensual and erotic work of sexual life, and all the sensual regressions which allow one to experience and enjoy life. The conditions and protocol of the sessions of psychoanalysis make it possible to construct and improve the spaces and paths of intimacy of each subject.

In psychoanalysis, candour does not only concern secrets and memories but also evokes in particular regressive unconscious wishes of all kinds, including those that are the most transgressive and that can only be known through interpretation.

DOI: 10.4324/9781032709819-14

The term *intimacy* thus refers as much to the proximity inside our consulting rooms as to the unconscious interiority of psychic life. By evoking candour and discretion, intimacy stands in contrast with the notions of public, social, and group life, which are much more evocative of education, diplomacy, and cautious freedom of thought than being in a state of latency. By requiring enunciation before reflection, the fundamental rule reverses the educational principle that requires children to think before they speak. The intimate speech of free association stands in opposition to civilised social speech. For its part, the analyst's listening is also freed from the putting into latency required by social life.

That is why it is interesting to compare our search for a singular intimacy, such as that of analytic sessions, with our gregarious propensity to establish organisations. These two fields correspond to two conflictual desires that both arise from the emergence of psychic life. As I have already pointed out, the latter requires the presence of a fellow human being who serves as a support for establishing thought processes by means of identification with the psychic processes of this other. This paradox whereby the growth of singular psychic life requires such a detour via another person is at the origin of all the conflicts between individual psychology and collective psychology, depending on whether this other is used as a vector or as an indispensable presence. In this case, the capacity to leave the group is reduced, and private intimacy is limited. *Private intimacy* is defined, then, by this capacity to leave the group, to break off the intimacies that are essential to its cohesion. We can easily see that certain difficulties encountered within our groups arise from failures in constructing and satisfying our intimate lives, or, to put it differently, that certain private infantile demands, with a transgressive potential, which have not been taken up during sessions due to a process of renunciation, are transferred on to group organisations insofar as these offer an easy and generic analogy with the family structures within which each child grows up. We then expect from institutions what they cannot give us; it is a matter of unconscious "false connections", and thus of *impossible expectations*, which are typical of every transference, hence the intensity of the disappointments, quarrels, and infighting which, in turn, can give rise to the disputes, confusions, and encysted controversies that sometimes result in ruptures and splits. Indeed, it is not uncommon for institutional conflicts to cover and conceal ethical problems, but also intrapsychic registers that continue to be transgressive. All those who have interested themselves in the history of our organisations have been astonished by the frequency of splits within groups of analysts. This congress is an opportunity to pursue certain paths of reflection linking private life and public life.

As I was writing these lines, I was thinking about several clinical facts which link this intimacy of analysis with group life within our psychoanalytic institutions. Candidates find that they are obliged, more or less, according to the training model used by their respective institutes, to include in their session discourse associations related to what they are experiencing within their institutes; the same is true for analysts who are already members of a society and who do a second analysis with an analyst who may or may not be from the same society as them. A difficulty arises here, as much for the analysand in maintaining free associative activity as for the analyst in maintaining evenly suspended attention. This clinical situation is connected with a much more general difficulty of analytic work bearing on ideologies, those that are implicit and private, certainly, but also those that are official, all of which are based on the infantile theories of the patient with whom the analyst is dealing. A particular feature of these ideologies and beliefs is that they are invested continuously and escape oscillations. They are opposed to regressions during the session and demand piety and fidelity. This difficulty of analysis is all the greater in that these ideologies are sustained by the societies to which we all belong, and often by their history, hence the tendencies to conformism and to the unconscious complicities, collusions, and consensus that are all based on alienating identifications. The analyst's neutrality, his or her evenly suspended attention, is thus not a given position but the result of his or her work of countertransference, including theoretical choices and personal commitments in his or her institution.

To come back now to intimacy. The meaning of this term remains linked to its etymology; *intimate* is the superlative of the Latin *interior* and means "what is innermost, at the centre". Generally, the topographical dimension of depth and background is associated with the idea of proximity, both with oneself and with others, but also with the idea of secret and inaccessibility, as well as with ideas of reserve and concealment. It is also associated with the idea of conviction, such as the intimate sense or conviction of an effective reality such as we have during our dreams, but which is also present in our beliefs and ideologies of all sorts, as well as our knowledge. The intimacy of our psychic functioning, this *"for intérieur"*, as we call it in French, or "innermost self", is closely linked with our hallucinatory system.

Much more than representations and precise contents, the notion of intimacy refers to a private subjective experience capable of being shared allusively without any need for explanation. The adherents of an ideology share the ideology which is based on a leader who upholds it, or on an idea and belief about what life is or what it should be like, a common *Weltanschauung* that they espouse together without enquiring into its meaning. Shared denials are based on such a use of language.

These considerations show that the initial empirical approach which posits an opposition between intimacy and the collective and makes intimacy depend on the capacity to break with the group is not sufficient for our theme. In effect, while certain forms of intimacy, those especially that involve our erogenous bodies, require us to leave the group mentally and physically, that is not the case for all of them. This rupture with the group, in fact, its putting into latency, is something evident where adult erotic life is concerned, but also where the acquisitions of childhood are concerned, such as cleanliness, bodily care, and bodily functions. At the same time as the body acquires its double valency as a social body and erogenous body, certain places become private spaces, which may or may not provide solitude: for instance, toilets, bathrooms, and bedrooms. The proximity of erogeneity, and of sensual regression, requires our social aspirations and the objects of the social domain to be put into latency. This aspect is particularly active during regression in the session.

Other forms of intimacy, on the contrary, are deployed within the group; they depend on and are reinforced by the fact of being shared with others – for example, religious feeling and, as its name indicates, communion, as well as certain collective rituals, but also all the exaltations and ideological beliefs which require and nourish the constitution of masses. What are the intimacies cultivated within our respective groups, and which private intimacies are excluded by the requirements of fidelity linked to membership of a group? Here there is a conflict between those forms of intimacy that are cultivated under the auspices of freedom of thought and those that are formed in the name of some sort of identificatory alienation within a group.

As I pointed out earlier, it is in this way that we can question the restrictive principles of psychoanalytic organisations that are not indispensable for the organisation of a group. One of the raisons d'être for our IMG is to try to understand how the history of each of our organisations can explain the difficulties that the organisation has encountered in the course of its development, in the aftermath of its foundations and vicissitudes, and more precisely, in the name of the implicit ideologies that it may conceal within it, sometimes since its origins, and which may have played a part in its very foundations.

You all know how difficult the terms *freedom* and *democracy* are to define, and how they imply very variable orientations, even though the terms themselves express universal individual and group aspirations; but their content is not difficult to define. We only need to think about the double meaning of the term *freedom*, that of gaining access to freedom of thought and that of freeing ourselves from the requirement to think. Similarly, we can content ourselves with the subtle contradiction of Churchill, for whom "[d]emocracy is the worst form of government, except for all the others". One of the advantages of having several training models is certainly that it reminds us that none of them is universal and totalitarian, that each one has its limits and its shortcomings, owing to its implicit implications.

It is the hallmark of certain words and expressions to sustain the register of collective psychology by transmitting a sufficiently vague and general meaning in which each person can recognise him- or herself without needing to specify the particular implications. Such is the case for the terms *freedom* and *democracy*, but also *intimacy*, as well as those of *depression, irritation, fatigue* – and no doubt other words in other languages – which we often hear in our sessions with the function of sidestepping the real issue, that is, of guaranteeing the repression of the individual elements concerned. Such terms from the collective domain place value on communitarianism and participate in the exclusion of private implications. Used in this way, they support the denial of differences, thereby confirming the idea that we are all the same. They thus satisfy the generic wish to be like everyone else, which is opposed to another equally generic wish, to be unique, to be the only and unique one.

Intimate is opposed, therefore, to *public* and not to group or social. The dialectic individual-group cannot be superimposed on that of intimate-public, and we cannot consider intimate and individual, group and public as equivalent. In fact, several forms of intimacy seem to exist, and the conflict shifts between private intimacies and group intimacies. This brings us back to a partial truth of my first proposition, but which is now enriched. Private intimacy rests on the capacity to leave the intimacy required by the group mentality. The faithful gather together in intimacy, in a common and shared intimacy, in which they fulfil the same unconscious wish hallucinatorily. It also brings us back to the logics of hysterical identification which, under the cover of a common shared experience, makes it possible to fulfil in a concealed way a singular Oedipal unconscious wish. In all groups, an intimate identification unites or binds together the members of the group.

The message transmitted by the word *intimacy* may thus be in apparent contradiction with the immediate sense of this term, which orients us deliberately towards the private. Intimacy can be a common identification with all the members of a group.

It is worth noting that Freud rarely uses the terms *intimacy* and *intimate*. In a speech given in 1926, he speaks of intimacy in connection with the motives of his affiliation with the Jewish people and mentality, namely, his Jewish identity (*identity* is another term of *communitarian psychology*), the absence of explanation regarding its individual significations being an implicit consensus:

> What bound me to Jewry was (I am ashamed to admit), neither faith nor national pride, for I have always been an unbeliever. . . . But plenty of other things remained over to make the attraction of Jewry and Jews irresistible – many obscure emotional forces, which were the more powerful the less they could be expressed in words, as well as a clear consciousness of inner identity, the safe privacy of a common mental construction.
>
> (Freud, 1941)

Again, what we find here is identification with the mental functioning of another person.

This identification is at the centre of our theme. It is indispensable for the establishment of individual psychic life. At the same time, it can be used at any moment to escape this process and to reinforce links with others instead of mental work, especially when such work is required, owing to affects of unpleasure. The inevitable conflict between individual psychology and collective psychology has its origins here. In fact, two modes of mental functioning are involved which are both linked to identification: one is subject to the most impersonal demands of the superego, and the other to the recourse to another person or other people, to the cultural superego. These two modes of functioning which are in conflict arise from the conditions of emergence of psychic life, which is achieved through the detour of identification with the *Nebenmensch*, with the risk of this identification being debased into an identification with a group sharing the same expectations towards the *Nebenmensch.*

The establishment of psychic life requires a transposition onto this other who will become at once an object of satisfaction, an object of hate, and a support of authority. Identification with the functioning of this other occurs in his presence through greed ("I want you"), and in his absence in order to reduce the unpleasure of the feeling of being excluded during his absence ("being like you," "I stay with you"). But this primal scene effect that is typical of absence also exists in presence.

The mental functioning of the other is perceived as unreachable, non-appropriable as such. The thought of the other becomes a primal scene of exclusion, eliciting in its turn an identification, with the thought of the other as an attempted ambivalent response. The tale of the goose with golden eggs is a fine illustration of the envy and hatred that great men can trigger in others due to their gifts and capacities. Identification makes it possible to be with another person mentally, but it also retains traces of exclusion and separation. It is born of hate and becomes the object of hate.

During the sessions, and beyond the pleasure of finding the past again, feelings of exclusion are actualised with their consequences, namely, experiences of abandonment, distress, sadness, and disdain. To avoid and escape these painful feelings of exclusion, patients repeat their childhood attempts to strengthen their ties and identifications within family relationships. As adults, they make use of group mentality and crowd ideologies; they restrict their own originality and reduce the regressive activities of their intimacy to conformism. In good cases, the transposition of these feelings and memories can take place in the transference of the analysis, but it can also take place in social, political, and religious organisations, and in particular for us in psychoanalytical institutions.

This experience of exclusion nourishes the transference of this identificatory quest from which individual and collective psychology, as well as singular intimacy and group mentality, will emerge. These two poles of identification can also be found within the psychoanalytic community, with the supporters of psychic work accusing the others of intersubjectivism and the latter accusing the former of solipsism. The conflict between private intimacy and group intimacy thus also overlaps with the conflict between the impersonal superego and the cultural superego that is active within the mind of every parent and hence transmitted to their children.

All this complicates the specific rules of management of organisations. The transference of authority, with tenderness and post-Oedipal firmness, can make way for many intense conflicts and crises and to the vicissitudes of authoritarian power, hate, splits, as well as inertia.

Intimacy consists, therefore, in being able to leave the intimacy of our groups and institutions, to the benefit of our private intimacies.

References

Freud, S. (1926). *Address to the Society of B'Nai B'Rith. SE* (Vol 20, pp. 271–274).
Freud, S. (1940/1938). *An outline of psychoanalysis. SE* (Vol. 23, pp. 139–208).
Freud, S. (1941). *Address to the society of B'nai B'rith, SE* (Vol. 20, pp. 273–274). (Original work published 1926)

Chapter 10

Could There Be Destructive Forces Vis-à-Vis Psychoanalysis Contained in the Intimate Workings of Psychoanalytical Societies?

Maggiorino Genta

General Historical Introduction

Shortly after the Nuremberg congress at the end of March 1910, in his text on "wild" analysis, Freud wrote:

> In the spring of 1910 we founded an International Psycho-Analytical Association, to which its members declare their adherence by the publication of their names, in order to be able to repudiate responsibility for what is done by those who do not belong to us and yet call their medical procedure "psycho-analysis". For as a matter of fact "wild" analysts of this kind do more harm to the cause of psycho-analysis than to individual patients.
>
> (Freud, 1910)

As suggested in 1912 by Jung, at that time president of the IPA, Freud recommended that "[e]veryone who wishes to carry out analysis on other people shall first himself undergo an analysis by someone with expert knowledge" (Ellenberger, 1994).

In 1918, at the Budapest congress, Dr Hermann Nunberg stated that "[n]o one should henceforth be allowed to analyze who himself had not been analyzed previously", a revolutionary idea at that time. In 1920, the Berlin Polyclinic and Institute was established, and Hanns Sachs became the first training analyst, with Franz Alexander the first student. In 1922, the Vienna Ambulatorium was established.

In 1925, at the Ninth International Congress, in Bad Homburg, Dr Max Eitingon made another controversial plea. He proposed the introduction of required and regular supervisions of analyses being conducted by student analysts. He suggested the establishment in each country of institutes especially concerned with training.

DOI: 10.4324/9781032709819-15

Almost one century after Numberg's and Eitingon's recommendations, there is still the same concern for the quality of psychoanalytic training and for the future of psychoanalysis.

In 1926, in *The Question of Lay Analysis*, whilst opposing the idea that the practice of analysis be reserved exclusively for doctors, Freud asserts that psychoanalysis should be "neither allowed, nor forbidden" and – above all – not be regulated by the state.

However, the newly created association needed to have rules for training and procedures for accreditation. What would be known as the "second fundamental rule", in other words, personal analysis, rapidly became a crucial question.

At first, it was enough for the interested party to attain a wider theoretical understanding by verifying the existence of the unconscious within himself. Thereafter, with the development of analytical technique and taking countertransference into account, one aimed for a "didactic analysis" as complete as possible.

According to existing models, one moves from the extreme of selection prior to any commitment, with highly organised courses by the institution, to the opposite extreme of post hoc admission, where the candidate assumes full responsibility for his own training.

The problem of the applicant's refusal to become a candidate remains present and current.

As Jean-Luc Donnet says on this issue, an institution defines itself as much by what it leaves "outside" as by what it takes "inside".

I wonder if the danger now is not towards a tendency to unhealthy conservatism which may result in rigidity and in a lack of openness to adaptive change.

I agree with Luiz Eduardo Prado de Oliveira when he says, "While psychoanalysis proceeds from an essentially revolutionary approach, it leads to the most conservative and reactionary forms of rigidity in all fields, which spring from the imprecise nature of its propositions" (2009).

Statistics of the Swiss Society (Showing How Much the Number of Candidates Is Decreasing)

First of all, I have to underline that the Swiss Society follows the French model for the training of candidates – that means that, before asking to be received as candidates, the applicant must have been engaged in a personal analysis with a member of our society, or with an IPA member of another society. As Kernberg says, "[t]he French model attempts to keep the candidate's analytic experience totally uncontaminated by institutional complications" (Kernberg, 2000).

Following the French model, the analyst does not give any information about his analysand but just the date of the beginning, and possibly of the ending, of the analysis.

As the selection of candidates takes place not at the start of their training but after an analytical experience, that can provide the faculty members who examine the prospective candidate with more realistic and tangible evidence of the potential candidate's capacity for analytic work, his analytic attitude, capacity for insight and introspection, intuitive grasping of unconscious material, and the extents to which potential "blind spots" have been resolved.

That also means that the average age of applicants may be close to 40, or even 50, when they ask to be received as candidates.

Until May 2017, analysis of four sessions a week was required, subsequent to the general assembly that took place on this date three sessions a week as recognised.

The Swiss Society, founded in 1919, has a reputation today for being very rigorous, to the point where the demand from future candidates has dropped considerably during the last 15 years, according to our most recent statistics. It is concerning this precise point that a debate could take place between colleagues from different societies, maybe particularly from old and young societies.

The following picture will show the situation of the Swiss Society:

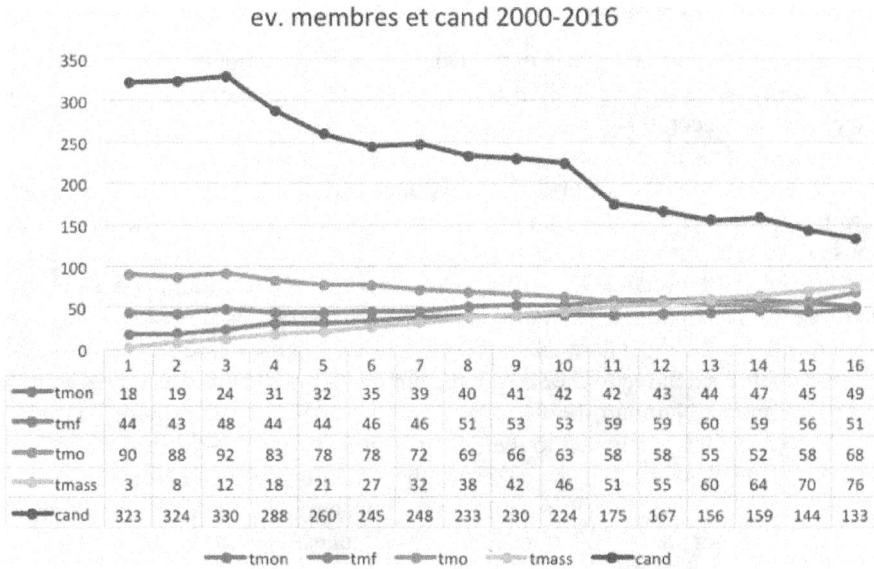

ev. membres et cand 2000-2016

	1	2	3	4	5	6	7	8	9	10	11	12	13	14	15	16
tmon	18	19	24	31	32	35	39	40	41	42	42	43	44	47	45	49
tmf	44	43	48	44	44	46	46	51	53	53	59	59	60	59	56	51
tmo	90	88	92	83	78	78	72	69	66	63	58	58	55	52	58	68
tmass	3	8	12	18	21	27	32	38	42	46	51	55	60	64	70	76
cand	323	324	330	288	260	245	248	233	230	224	175	167	156	159	144	133

tmon   tmf   tmo   tmass   cand

Figure 10.1 Members and candidates, Swiss Society, 2000–2016.

Note: The upper **blue line** indicates tendency of candidate applications, since 2000, comparing with honorary members (sky-blue line), training members (red line), full members (grey line), and associated members (yellow line).

cand 2001 -2016

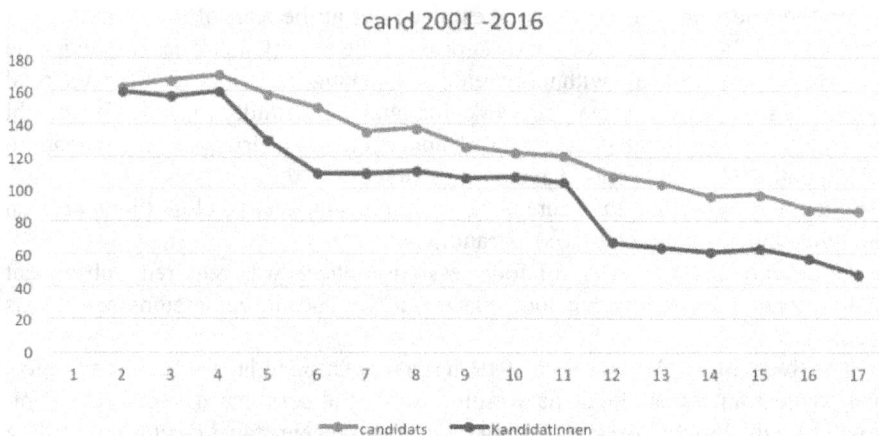

Figure 10.2 Candidates, Swiss Society, 2001–2016.

Note: Blue line indicates candidates from French-speaking Switzerland; red line candidates from German-speaking Switzerland.

Destructive Forces?

I ask myself the following question: "Does not the institutional space for admission, which should remain flexible and regulated at the same time, sometimes have a tendency to become rigid, particularly in older societies? Have the criteria for being accepted as a candidate by a society become more and more demanding?"

Having a look at the history, very old papers, from the 1950s and 1960s, concerning this problem of accepting candidates seems to indicate that criteria were not so rigid as in the 1990s, or as now . . .

Since its institutionalisation in the 1920s, psychoanalytical training has become increasingly systematised, formalised, and broadened. During the initial phase, selection was, for the most part, taken for granted. During the phase that began in the late forties and extended to the sixties, the approach to selection became generally more systematic (Namnun, 1980).

This movement was linked to the fact that, little by little, at the end of the Second World War, psychoanalysis gained high professional status and psychiatrists, in increasing numbers, began to apply for psychoanalytical training for reasons of prestige and academic, social, or economic advantages. The question of motivation became a complex one.

As the question of an applicant's motivation for a psychoanalytical career has become more complex and can no longer be taken for granted, it has come to be one of the principal areas of interest for admissions committees. The pathology of applicant and its relation to their motivation has become another primary area of interest.

In my review of the literature, I found that the Fifth IPA Conference of Training Analysts took place here, in Buenos Aires, in July 1991, under the chairmanship of Otto Kernberg, with the title "Between Chaos and Petrification: Problems in the

Integration of Different Theoretics-Clinical Frameworks in the Formation of the Psychoanalysts".

Different presentations were given, and it is amazing to note that the most conservative one, as Wallerstein says in his paper (1993), was by Janice de Saussure, from Geneva. She underlined nevertheless "the need to evaluate carefully the capacities of candidates at different stages in their development", which, as a matter of fact, is not really done at present in our society.

André Green of Paris, on the contrary, affirmed:

[A]n explicit preoccupation with the deforming presence of power within the structure of organised psychoanalytical training, the pathology of power, with all its correlates of coerced dogmatism, enforced infantilisation and narcissistic aggrandizement of those who hold and deploy power, that is inherent within any hierarchical and bureaucratic organisation.

Some others were surprised that students are not more rebellious. "Have we created organisations which promote unnaturally passive acceptance in the students?" they wondered.

But Green concluded on a personal note, and I quote: "I realize that I cannot recommend to others anything different from what I have myself endeavoured to do in my own work."

The most radical critique of our training programs was given by André Lussier, who talked about "[t]he stifling rigidity, the suffocating indoctrination, our failure to attract enough creative candidates, the pathogenic effects, *intra muros*, of the non-analyzed transference and counter-transference with their cortege of idealisation and paranoid attitude, etc." And also that "[t]he quest for freedom seems to be frequently mistaken for chaos or treated as adolescent rebelliousness".

Otto F. Kernberg wrote ironically (1996) a very interesting paper with the title "Thirty ways to destroy creativity of psychoanalytic candidates".

After having heard a colleague say to him, "Our problem is not so much to foster creativity but to try not to inhibit the creativity, naturally stimulated by the nature of our work", Kernberg wrote this paper, presenting, in a negative format, what is essentially a plea for the fostering of psychoanalytic creativity.

This paper is concerned primarily with new candidates, but we also find the way through which new applicants can be discouraged from the idea of becoming a candidate or do not insist on being admitted as a candidate.

For example: "Slow down the processing of applications; delay accepting candidates; slow down the providing of information to candidates: this will help to slow them down in turn."

And also:

It may be very helpful to point out that psychoanalysis is understood and carried out properly only in places far away from your own institution, and preferably in a language not known by many of your students. If the demands of the training are such that the students would not be able to spend an extended part of the time in that distant ideal land, they may become convinced that it is useless to attempt to develop psychoanalytic science in a place so far from where the true and only theory and technique are taught. And that conviction will last.

In the Swiss Society, which follows the French model, German applicants may have this feeling, as the French part of the society is very oriented toward the French Societies. And we saw in our picture number 2 that the number of German candidates, as indicated by the red line, continues to decrease.
Finally:

Make sure that some unusually critical or rebellious candidates who threaten the atmosphere of harmony at seminars, challenge their senior instructors or dare to talk publicly against training analysts in the presence of their analysands (likely, of course, to report such conversations in their sessions) are gently kept back or stimulated to resign.

In 1995 another interesting paper was presented at the 39th IPA conference in San Francisco and published two years later: "The historical roots of psychoanalysis orthodoxy".
The author concludes that:

Freud believed that psychoanalysis, an empirical science free from the need for a priori certainty, could dispense with philosophical assumptions. This turned out not to be so. Freud, as well as every heretic and modifier, bases his ideas on a view of the nature of man, which cannot be proven or disproven by data obtained in the psychoanalytic interview.

(Bergmann, 1997)

And also:

Every psychoanalyst who listens to free associations and other data to organise what he hears into a structure more coherent than that available to the analysand. Such an organisation is not possible without a pre-existing model in the mind of the analyst . . .
  Some measure of tradition or orthodoxy is therefore inevitable. We are therefore dealing with a paradox: every analyst needs a cohesive model from which to make his interpretations. On the other hand, his skill as an analyst is increased if he can draw upon other models to meet the needs of a particular analysand.

(ibid.)

Selection of Candidates, an Old Problem in the History of Psychoanalysis

We can recognise that all societies in the world think that the selection of candidates is a central problem.

Several authors criticise the significantly increasing conformism. And at the same time, psychoanalysis itself is generally criticised, as having the tendency to normalise people someway in a social order.

Often, our committees for selection of candidates select conformist applicants more readily and reject the non-conformist ones.

As if we were afraid to receive in our societies members that could, in the future, perturb or provoke trouble. At the same time, by the way, we have to admit also that often real progress in psychoanalysis came much more from original and non-conformist members.

In some way, our "serious" training analysts have been chosen to make training, as if we do not trust "original" training analysts, that have relationships which are not so politically correct.

A. Green, for the problem of selection of candidates, considered in an interesting paper, "Artisans are preferred to artists" (1973).

Which Criteria?

Aptitude for psychoanalysis cannot be strictly defined because of its wide range.

In the literature, it is generally underlined that the selection of candidates for psychoanalytic training is one of the most important and vulnerable spots in the establishment of psychoanalytic educational programs.

Since its institutionalisation in the 1920s, psychoanalytic training has become increasingly systematised, formalised, and broadened. During the phase that began in the late forties and extended to the sixties, the approach to selection became generally more systematic.

We may stress that many papers in the forties, fifties, and sixties indicate general criteria that do not seem to be so difficult to achieve.

In the early sixties, it was admitted in New York that

the acceptable candidate is a young physician who is a sound psychiatric clinician, whose emotional conflicts are within the sphere of reversible pathology, whose intelligence has that intangible capacity for intuitive apperception of unconscious process which always include a sincere interest in cultural pursuits and the humanities. As he is imaginative and sensitive of his own feelings, he is intuitive of the feelings of others, and he is sufficiently articulate that this awareness can be expressed in meaningful language.

(Eisendorfer, 1959)

Several writers (Greenacre, 1961) were in general accord with the basic requirements of intelligence, honesty, and sufficient educational and cultural background, such as would be necessary for the pursuit of any profession.

The special qualities mentioned as important for an analyst were sustained curiosity about behaviour and mental activities of human beings; respect for others; some aptitude in accessing the unconscious; love and persistent pursuit of the truth; a modest degree of creativity, or at least a creative appreciation; and capacity for reflexion and introspection, in contrast to a habitual demand for action. And also, the most frequent opinion was that the neurosis, provided it could be analysed, was not a handicap in training but might furnish effective motivation and add to psychoanalytic sensitivity!

Some other papers (Langer, 1964) in the early sixties, during a period with a big development of psychoanalysis, indicate that in the selection of candidates, training analysts must take care that the applicant has a real interest for psychoanalysis and is not an opportunist that would become an analyst just because this is a good way to gain a lot of money – times have certainly changed!

About this topic, Anna Freud said:

If you want to be a real psychoanalyst you must have a great love for truth, scientific truth as well as personal truth, and you have to place this appreciation of truth higher than any discomfort at meeting unpleasant facts, whether they belong to the world outside or to your own inner person.

(1967)

In our society, anyone wishing to be admitted to psychoanalytical training must of course submit to a stringent selection procedure. This was not the case in the early years of psychoanalysis, when motivation was all that was required.

Today, every training institute will endeavour to train candidates in such a way that they become good psychoanalysts. But who is to define that concept? What makes someone a good psychoanalyst?

I wonder if we are not selecting for something we cannot really describe. And anyway, nothing can be predicted about events in the applicant's life. Selection involves attempting a statement about a future expectation. We cannot know how the applicant will have developed in six or seven years.

Finally, selection for psychoanalysis training means selection without a clear description of the concept of "a good analyst" and without the possibility of evaluating the selection process. If the problem is put in these terms, it seems almost absurd to retain selection.

Would it not be better to formulate requirements for admission and then admit everyone who satisfies them?

It is often stated in the literature that selection is performed on the basis of the selector's own criteria, on a "like me" basis: "For better and for worse the interviewer has to compare the candidate with himself" (Bird, 1968).

In my opinion, it should not be essential for the applicant already to possess the characteristics required to be a "good analyst".

During the period I have been working in the selection committee, I have often had the impression that in our society some selectors sometimes had this kind of expectation. The question is whether or not it is possible to predict that the applicant will have developed the qualities of a "good analyst" by the end of his training.

Concerning the situation of statistics of our society, I wonder if the selection criteria have not been too strict, so that a number of good candidates have been unjustifiably turned away.

Naturally, selectors can differ widely in their selection methods. Differences that are very difficult to objectify.

In the literature, various selection methods, including even psychological testing, have been tested elsewhere and abandoned again. Interviewing remains the most widely used instrument.

But no definition of a "good analyst" exists, nor is there any testable method of selection.

Several authors agree that "[i]n selecting for psychoanalytical training, we are doing something we do not (precisely) know in order to achieve something we cannot (precisely) describe" (Kappelle, 1996).

Would it be possible to limit a selection procedure to a consideration of the applicant's personal analysis and a judgement of his or her positive achievements up to that point of his or her life?

Once more, we can ask to ourselves if, in our society, we are too rigid and demanding to an applicant who desires to be admitted as candidate.

I really think we have the reputation that it is very difficult to be admitted, and so several potential applicants prefer to renounce psychoanalytical training. Often, when I took part in the training committee of our society, I had the impression that, in some way, the applicants were requested to be psychoanalysts already, even before having started their training.

A Suggestion

As Winnicott says, patients are our best teachers. I wonder whether they could also be, in some way, our best supervisors.

Why must we be so demanding as, anyway, a candidate that is not a good one will not be able to find patients? I wonder if it would be more useful to be a little bit less demanding and trust the fact that, beyond our appreciation, a good candidate will be able to find patients for analysis and a bad one finally will not.

Conclusion

Psychoanalysis is currently under powerful attack within our culture and within the university, particularly from the viewpoint of a strong biologically oriented psychiatry and a cognitive/behaviourally oriented clinical psychology.

Furthermore, I think that – even if it is possible to detect these attacks and crises within certain societies – analytical thinking is still very much alive.

References

Bergmann, M. (1997). The historical roots of psychoanalytical orthodoxy. *International Journal of Psychoanalysis*, *78*, 69–86.

Bird, B. (1968). On candidate selection and its relation to analysis. *International Journal of Psychoanalysis*, *49*, 513–527.

Eisendorfer, A. (1959). The selection of candidates applying for psychoanalytic training. *Psychoanalytic Quarterly*, *28*, 374–378.

Ellenberger, H. (1994). *Histoire de la découverte de l'inconscient*. Fayard.

Freud, S. (1910). *'Wild' psycho-analysis. SE* (Vol. 11, pp. 219–228).

Freud, A. (1967). The evaluation of applicants for psychoanalytical training. *International Journal of Psychoanalysis, 49*, 553.

Green, A. (1973). Quelques remarques sur la formation des psychanalystes. *Bulletin, 3*, 5–10.

Greenacre, P. (1961). A critical digest of the literature on selection of candidates for psychoanalytic training. *The Psychoanalytic Quarterly, 30*, 28–55.

Kappelle, W. (1996). How useful is selection. *International Journal of Psychoanalysis, 77*, 1213–1232.

Kernberg, O. (1996). Thirty ways to destroy creativity of psychoanalytic candidates. *International Journal of Psychoanalysis, 77*(5), 1031–1040.

Kernberg, O. (2000). A concerned critique of psychoanalytical education. *International Journal of Psychoanalysis, 81*(1), 97–120.

Langer, M. (1964). Critères de selection applicables à la formation des étudiants en psychanalyse. *RFP, 28*(1), 7–16.

Namnun, A. (1980). Trends in the selection of candidates for psychoanalytical training. *Journal of the American Psychoanalytic Association, 28*, 419–437.

Oliveira, L. P. O. (2009). La formations des psychanalystes et leurs institutions. In *Les pires ennemis de la psychanalyse: Contribution à l'histoire de la critique interne*. Liber.

Wallerstein, R. (1993). Between chaos and petrification: A summary of the fifth IPA conference of training analysts. *International Journal of Psychoanalysis, 74*, 165–178.

Part V

Institutional Life in Psychoanalytic Organisations

Chapter 11

The Many Facets of Authority in Psychoanalytic Institutions

Jasminka Šuljagić

In his inaugural lecture of literary semiotics chair of the College de France, delivered on 7 January 1977, Roland Barthes gives to the projected experience the name "Sapientia". He says that this experience has an ancient and currently unfashionable name, which he would dare to take at the intersection of its etymology: "Sapientia: no power, a little knowledge, a little wisdom, and as much savour as possible" (Barthes, 1979). A few days after his inaugural lecture, Barthes starts his lectures titled "Comment vivre ensemble" ("How to live together").

What is the name of that experience of working together in our psychoanalytic institutions?

Might we say that we enter and become part of them with well-deserved serene joy, equipped for open enquiry, ready for further changes?

How does our institutional history find its place here? Have we taken it over, with all its unique characteristics, to an extent that even it allows us to forget about it?

Are the authorities, those who teach us and those who lead us, placed where they belong?

Would we rather be the "professor's guests", at Prof. Freud's home every Wednesday evening at eight thirty, than members of an organisation?

Overview

The concept of authority initially eludes us. We recognise it either as a negative and an absence or as an overemphasised, perverted presence. Our claim is that "[t]here is no such thing as authority" (Foucault, 1980); "we are no longer in a position to know what authority really is" (Arendt, 1961); "the actual essence of this phenomenon has rarely attracted any attention" (Kojeve, 2014). It is like some kind of phantom that no one believes in any longer but whom many fear – frightening others as well, by recalling the possible outcomes of its sudden revival, together with what is more tangible and familiar: power, violence, or force.

There is some form of disappearance that we lament, as well as the discomfort of coming to terms with our own indifference and our own disdain.

If we accept some of the designations of this concept and agree that it may be considered as the possibility of an act, followed by voluntarily refraining from

DOI: 10.4324/9781032709819-17

reacting to it, or as obedience in which freedom is retained, what becomes noticeable is the intertwining of the possibilities of action and abstention, of freedom and its limits. It is important that we keep our attention on this voluntary limitation of our own freedom, on the framework for its existence and flourishing. It could be expected that this duality is well known to us and that we have found a way to combine these two possible moves and are able to accept this duality in all its forms, where the setting is merely one, the most visible one. In other words: that we are capable of maintaining the validity of this concept in its proper sense.

Is that, indeed, the case?

Authors and Authorities: The Foundations

The concept of authority, in its original meaning, can be traced back to the founding of ancient Rome (Arendt, 1961), as part of the belief in the sacredness of foundation. Once something is built, it remains binding. The foundations are set, and they should therefore be preserved – "adding, as it were, to every single moment the whole weight of the past. . . [a]nything that happened was transformed into an example" (ibid., p. 123). The Latin word "auctoritas" derives from the verb "augere" – to multiply, augment – and indeed, the foundations are constantly augmented. "Auctor" – originator, promoter – bears that burden, solemnly and seriously.

In one of his first playful letters to his friend Eduard Silberstein, Freud notes: "An old superstition has it that no building is sound whose foundations have not cost a human sacrifice" (Boehlich, 1990, cited in Grosskurth, 1991, p. 33). Many other foundation myths speak of this, among others the one related to Rome, where the dispute over whether the city should be founded on Palatine Hill or Aventine Hill arises, and where criticism, derision, and the first leap over the wall end in murder: "So perish every one that shall hereafter leap over my wall."

It may be important to explore the origins of our particular psychoanalytic institutions, not only the hills on which they were built, but also the hills on which they might have been built but were not. It is possible that there, in the very foundations, in the barely visible yet raging differences between the founders, lie the roots of later rifts which subsequently continued to replicate themselves and grow increasingly more intricate. Who saw 6 birds, and who saw 12 birds? Who saw them first from his own sacred place?[1] Or is it merely an echo, the repetition of an old battle fought two generations back, when King Numitor was dethroned by his own brother, before Romulus and Remus were even born? Then there is also the subsequently often neglected passion of beginnings, the joy of creation, the zest and momentum of something new, of love. In every foundation, the hope and anticipation of an imagined promise is also a glimpse into the future.

With their very presence, organisations bear all the passionate feelings of those who belong to them. Authorities, in the proper sense of the word, whether professional or organisational, are the ones that enable and allow this, in the course of new changes with growing complexity.

The increasing foundations of Freud's discoveries brought the need for the constant enlargement of the structure and organisation, starting from the first "congresses", as Freud jokingly called his encounters with Fliess, and the first meetings with Stekel, Adler, Kahane, and Reitler in 1902 (denoting the foundation of the Psychological Wednesday Society, which changed its name to the Vienna Psychoanalytic Society), all the way to the first real congress in Salzburg, 1908 and the second one in Nuremberg, 1910, with the foundation of the International Psychoanalytic Association (IPA), followed by the establishment of yet one more organisation in 1912 – the Secret Committee.

Each of these foundational acts was, at the same time, a new opportunity to enthral and inspire exchanges and discoveries ("One could really learn from everyone", stated Ferenczi, in his letter to Freud after the Nuremberg Congress; Ferenczi, 1910, p. 157) and was also a new barrier against growing rivalries, envies, and hostilities.

"No idea may be used without the authorisation of its author." "Personal invectives and attacks should immediately be suppressed by the Chairman who shall be given authority to do so." Those were the proposals which, according to the minutes of the Vienna Psychoanalytic Society (Nunberg & Federn, 1962, cited in Eisold, p. 90), could be heard at the group's Wednesday meeting of 5 February 1908. They are seen as the origins of a bigger structure and organisation – making the informal group into a psychoanalytical society – as an attempt to overcome the sense of disquiet following the announcement of the first international congress and the formation of a larger international group. This is a touching historical snapshot, a moment of longing for a tougher authority under the sudden threat of its loss in a period complacently forgetful of its presence.

Although these proposals were not accepted at that time, the establishment of the IPA two years later helped structure the Vienna Psychoanalytic Society and the appointment of Adler as its president. A bit later, in 1912, it was the departure of Adler, followed by Stekel, with Jung showing signs of going the same way, which provided the impetus that led to the formation of the "Secret Committee", separated from the IPA, and consisting of Freud's closest, fully trusted associates. This was the period when Freud was writing *Totem and Taboo* (1913).

The inevitable alternation of creation and dissolution, sometimes to the very brink of survival.

In the summer of 1907, Freud announced that he had dissolved the society, giving each member the opportunity to renew membership (Nunberg & Federn, 1962).

In November 1913, Ferenczi wrote to Freud: "We don't get anything out of the International Association. Its dissolution will be a deliverance" (Ferenczi, 1913, p. 519).

In 1919, Jones dissolved the London Society and founded the British Society with "an improved membership" (Paskauskas, 1993, p. 328).

All of us, as members of psychoanalytic societies, bear witness to the history of numerous break-ups which have paradoxically and painfully sometimes been the only way to keep and develop what we already have. If authorities are those who found and keep what has been created, we could, and one might say that even in this context we should, ask ourselves: Why is that so hard?

The Preservation

At times, we are bewildered. We argue that it is our duty to safeguard Freud's legacy, to preserve the psychoanalytic tradition as an obligation to the founding father. But then we are concerned that this might reveal an apostle-like mentality and/or Messianic approach, and we continue stating that no one has been given the right or the capacity to do so. We are saying that our organisations should not operate according to a political but to a scientific model, although we are not sure what "scientific" actually means. We feel that we should avoid using the term "psychoanalytic movement". In the small number of existing texts on our institutions, we relentlessly search for weak points in their functioning and then say that we are "children of a fatherless family", and that we have no one to show us the way. Sometimes, we firmly believe that we are the ones who know what the truth is, and we fight fierce battles with anyone who advocates a different truth. Sometimes, our authorities are elsewhere – neurosciences, governmental and health delivery systems, or public opinion.

This is not only a question of whether we are now authorised to know and whether we are the legitimate heirs of Freud's creation but also a question of the creation itself, and its very nature.

> To say that Freud founded psychoanalysis does not (simply) mean that we find the concept of the libido or the technique of dream analysis in the works of Karl Abraham, or Melanie Klein; it means that Freud made possible a certain number of divergences – with respect to his own texts, concepts and hypotheses – that all arise from the psychoanalytic discourse itself.
>
> (Foucault, 1969, p. 131)

According to this view, Freud is a unique, uncommon author, together with Marx – "the founder of discursivity" – not just the author of his own work. He established an endless possibility of discourse, the possibilities and rules for the formation of other texts. He, like a novelist, opened the way not only for a certain number of similarities and analogies but also for a certain number of differences.

Also, it is not the same as with the founder of a science. In science, the act that founds it is on equal footing with its future transformation, and it becomes part of the set of modifications.

In contrast, in "our science", initiation is heterogeneous to future transformations and does not participate in them.

Freud thus created a possibility for something other than his work yet something belonging to what he founded. This duality is binding, leading us both to preserve and develop it, and it is similar to the already-established polarity of obedience and freedom. Our development also always involves a "return to the origins", and our authorities are those who make this movement possible. It is not just a mere addition to our starting point – an endless, linear sequence – but rather a series of transformations continually changing and modifying it.

In the ancient drama *Oedipus at Colonus*, our hero, Oedipus, at the end of his life's path, meets another hero, Theseus, whose name has the same root as the Greek word θεσμός, thesmós – "institution", "organisation".

The Athenians of that time saw Theseus as the "forefather" and "founder", a legendary Athenian leader from the old, heroic epochs, the one who brought them together as a supreme traditional authority. This encounter deserves complete dramatisation and requires a stage.[2]

"Tell me" (*Oedipus at Colonus*, Project Gutenberg, adapted[3]) are the words with which Theseus addresses the aged, blind, outcast, homeless, and polluted Oedipus. "And therefore know you, son of Laius" (ibid.). Theseus knows that Oedipus is a wandering, blind beggar and also the one who saved and led Thebes. He himself, in an astonishing interplay of mythical similarities, albeit rather mitigated in comparison with Oedipus's fate, had been deserted by his father, learnt about his origins at one point, fought dangerous monsters in search of his father, and unknowingly contributed to his death.

In this encounter, Oedipus gains recognition, acceptance, sanctuary, and a final resting place. This acceptance is not quite like the days of yore, from King Polybus and Queen Merope in the city of Corinth. Much was to transpire in the meantime, and now, before his encounter with Theseus, Oedipus is exposed to repeated demands for a retelling of these events:

Ha! Where is he? Look around! . . . Who can he be – Zeus save us! – this old man? . . . Wanderer, now you are at rest, tell me of your birth and home, from what far country are you come? . . . Say on. How so? How? . . . The tale is bruited far and near, and echoes still from ear to ear, the truth, I fain would hear.

(chorus, ibid.)

Here he will also be faced with the social order he belongs to and with his place in the community. All this is happening at a place sacred to the Furies, female chthonic deities of vengeance. Soon enough we will learn that the second crossroads are nearby as well, and with Theseus's entrance, the lamenting verse turns into iambic trimeter.

Theseus, being a foreigner himself, accepts that which is foreign. In times to come, Oedipus's resting place will be known to nobody but himself and his successors. He was the only one who witnessed it, "with upraised hand, shading his eyes as from some awful sight, that no man might endure to look upon" (ibid.). Thereby, according to the oracle's foretelling, he inherits some strange and undescribed gift – the grave of Oedipus will bring great rewards to the city and be a blessing to the land in which it is situated. In Sophocles's drama, this is the way to preserve the city – "Thus shall you hold this land inviolate" (ibid.).

The Succession and the Vicissitudes

In his efforts to preserve what had been created, psychoanalysis as a "valuable part of reality" (Freud, 1925, p. 51), Freud was repeatedly faced with difficulties in its transmission. Such passion and hope, bitterness and resignation can be found in this act of tirelessly searching for someone who would take over and continue his work. And therefore he writes, not only the story of Oedipus facing the misfortune of a patricide, but also about the mythical times of the primal horde and of the killing of the primeval father. All foundational acts based on violence and crime, always expressing the same powerful love and hatred, admiration and rebelliousness – these are the oscillations which Freud sees as fundamental phenomena of our emotional life, and at one point he also assigns to them this particular place as their origin.

They further unfold, in the mythical past in totem feasts, through a plethora of sounds, movements, and colours, all of which follow the initial stillness. The clan celebrates the "cruel slaughter of its totem animal and is devouring it raw – blood, flesh and bones" (Freud, 1913, p. 139). Then there is lamenting and bewailing, followed by excessive, boundless, festive rejoicing – the glorification of taking into themselves the sacred life which reinforces their identification with him and with one another.

And lest we forget, here is something we will come back to later:

> Thus it became a duty to repeat the crime of parricide again and again in the sacrifice of the totem animal, whenever, as a result of the changing conditions of life, the cherished fruit of the crime – appropriation of the paternal attributes – threatened to disappear.
>
> (ibid., p. 144)

As the story unfolds, we witness the elevation of the murdered father into a god, and one quite astonishing scene of the twofold presence of the father: during the sacrifice before the god of the clan, the father is, in fact, represented twice over – as both god and as the totemic animal victim. Here, the defeat and vanquish of the father are, at the same time, an inalienable part of the presentation of his ultimate triumph.

What follows is an increasing departure from the totemic: a previous father substitute now moves towards gods and kings, while "the two driving factors", says Freud, "the son's sense of guilt and the son's rebelliousness, never become extinct" (ibid., p. 151).

The converging point in which the senses of guilt and rebellion become counterparts relative to the voluntary obedience and freedom was mentioned at the beginning as composite determinants of the notion of authority. Any further consideration of the topic of authority may now seem as a passage between two massive building blocks – the description of religions on one side, and huge authoritative powers on the other.

It is time for us to stop briefly in order to take a look at different sociological theories on the role of power in the determination of authority and the concept of power itself.

Ultimately, this is an issue of whether authority and power are mutually exclusive – "The most conspicuous characteristic of those in authority is that they do not have power" (Arendt 1961) – or so inextricable that one cannot be understood without the other – "Authority is the power accepted as legitimate by those subjected to it" (Weber, 1968).

Furthermore, the question is whether power, as the position to carry out one's own will – despite resistance – necessarily includes domination and subordination (ibid.), with the inevitable temptation to expand power beyond its legitimate spheres (de Jouvenal, 1962). Or are there some forms of cooperative and non-dominative power – power with and not just power over (Parsons, 1991)? Perhaps an increase in power for one person or group need not imply a decrease in power for others (ibid.); perhaps power is a two-way relational reality, a network in which everyone is the authority, where, besides being repressive, there is another approach to power as a productive force (Foucault, 1980).

This duality was present, in a noticeable form, as early as in Plato's efforts to introduce a kind of authority into the public life of the ancient polis. There is the allegory of the cave, of ideas as standards and measures – for the few; and the myth of hell, of rewards and punishment in the hereafter – for the many. Let us remember that the encounter between Oedipus and Theseus – as the protector – happens at a place sacred to the Furies, those deities of vengeance, and that Oedipus carries both a blessing and a curse.

These are all various forms of the polarity that are well known to us: the ego ideal and a critical agency (Freud, 1914), the superego with functions of prohibition and ideal (Freud, 1923), the superego and ego ideal. From different perspectives, these are more or less united, sometimes presented through a number of successive scenes (dual origin of the superego), sometimes concurrently in only one (god and totem animal in the totem feast; division of the ego in melancholia or in delusions of being watched), more or less in harmony with each other. The superego alone, with its various functions, is perceived as inseparable from a vicissitude of the Oedipus complex, with greater emphasis on castration anxiety (Freud, 1924, 1926), or on ambivalence (Freud, 1923), or as an archaic, pre-genital superego, terrifying and tormenting (Klein, 1932).

The Authorities We Allow Them to Be

In *Group Psychology and the Analysis of the Ego* (1921), Freud writes about how an individual gives up his ego ideal and substitutes for it the group ideal as embodied in the leader, which enables mutual identification among the members of the group and the reversal of initially hostile feelings into a positively toned relation. He then goes a step further: "The leader of the group is still the dreaded primal father; the group still wishes to be governed by unrestricted force; it has an extreme passion for authority. . . . [I]t has a thirst for obedience" (ibid.).

If we re-read Bion's *Experiences in Groups* (1961), we will be impressed and amused by his descriptions of the group "wait[ing] for the group to begin": the silence, the pressure, and the expectation of him to do something, indignation at his failure to appreciate that the group is entitled to expect something from him, the emergence of temporary leaders, gloomy thoughts about the disruption of the group, even coaxing him to mend his ways, all the way to growing discomfort. "I am certain that the group is quite unable to face the emotional tensions within it without believing that it has some sort of God who is fully responsible for all that takes place" (ibid.).

Once established, the authorities are faced with a multitude of temptations and challenges.

In our psychoanalytic institutions, with their unique origins and manner of transmission, there are inevitable issues concerning the right to train, the nature of the knowledge to be transmitted, and the method for doing it, as well as the questions – who is the authority that will now determine what psychoanalysis is, and what should we do once we have figured this out? This is an area which has been dealt with the most in the scarce literature on psychoanalytic institutions and in ever-present gossip – we hear and read about the authoritarian approach, the bureaucratisation of psychoanalysis, passionate power struggles over training issues, and about unfree associations.

Without disregarding the significance of the present viewpoint, we can consider this from another perspective. We no longer have taboos by which we guard our authorities or against which we guard ourselves, which Freud speaks about, according to Frazer. But that does not mean that we do not mould them to meet our needs. Freud's reputation as the tyrannical father who could not let his sons grow up to become independent is well known to us. However, in November 1910, Freud himself complained to Jung about his growing difficulties with Adler: "He is . . . forcing me into the unwelcome role of the aging despot who prevents young men from getting ahead" (cited in Eisold, 1997). In April 1910, he wrote to Ferenczi that he felt threatened by "falling into the role of the dissatisfied and superfluous old man" (ibid.). Although we are trained to follow those forces in our analytic work without having to respond to them instantly, it is more difficult, even impossible, to do that in our institutional life. We expect, often naively, that there will be no such forces there, or that the initial urge to have a leader will be justified by the group's focus on its purpose, or by the distribution of tasks and full commitment to them, not to mention gratitude. But always anew, we are faced with the clear acknowledgement of the necessity to have authorities also making clear efforts to disprove them. Perhaps all these are just ways to "repeat the crime of parricide again and again" (Freud, 1913), on a small scale, with an outcome known to us as the crisis of or disappearance of authority. The legitimacy of tradition that authority rests upon can easily turn into conservative resistance to development, while hope becomes an illusion that development can be avoided.

From two different theoretical perspectives, we learn about some of the manoeuvres a group may use to achieve this. Chasseguet-Smirgel (1985) writes about the fusion between the ego and the ideal, whereby the father figure, the superego, as the mature ego ideal, is violently and completely set aside. The group leader is the one who maintains the illusion of the reunification of the ego and the ego ideal by the shortest route, without any waiting, mental efforts, and development. This is also the basis of an egalitarian theory where all differences are erased, and the group is not organised around the leader but around the group itself, a group which is self-generated. Bion (1961) writes about some groups' objections to the assumption that they were brought together for the purpose of carrying out a task, about the demand for magic, with the leader as a magician. With "the hatred for learning by experience", the group yearns for the state in which it could be equipped for life without the need for any development or learning, with a boyish belief in a hero who never does any work but is always perfectly equipped.

What happens within the horde after the murder of the father, besides the fact that this act must be repeated, through totem meals, in order to regain "the cherished fruit of the crime – appropriation of the paternal attributes" (Freud, 1913)? Sons cannot use what caused the murder to occur, and none of them ever becomes the father who was removed.

Was du ererbt von deinen Vätern hast,
Erwirbes, um eszubesitzen.[4]

What from your fathers' heritage is lent,
Earn it anew, to really possess it!
(Faust, Project Gutenberg)

Without much elaboration, Freud quotes these verses on two occasions. Besides the repeated crime of patricide, this is another way to appropriate the paternal attribute. In it, this act itself is contained and transformed, not by mere repetition, but in a process of work and working through – a process that is seldom quiet and composed.

Before we finish, let us take one brief look at the question from the beginning.

Guest – Members

At the previously mentioned psychological society group's Wednesday meeting in February 1908, the following comment was also heard: "We are no longer the type of gathering we once were. Although we are still guests of the Professor, we are about to become an organisation" (Nunberg & Federn, 1967, cited in Eisold, 1994). Subsequently, in April 1910, after the Nuremberg congress and the establishment of the IPA, the following finally became clear: "Until now, the members of the Society have been his guests: now this is no longer feasible. The society must constitute itself and elect a president" (ibid.). And the newly elected president, Adler, stated: "We can therefore say today that from now on we belong to an association that chooses its president in a free election by members, with equal rights, like every other association" (ibid.).

From then onwards, we are compelled by the urge to be "like every other association" and still remain guests, if this is in any way possible – guests at their own homes. In accordance with this demand, we still mould our life within psychoanalytic communities and our authorities who, occasionally, address us with the question: "What can we do for you, dear guests?" This is a question we expect, and while in our guestly slumber, we disregard it and we consent to it.

Notes

1 In the myth on the founding of Rome, Romulus and Remus could not agree on its location; Romulus preferred the Palatine Hill. Remus preferred the Aventine Hill. They agreed to seek the will of the gods in this matter, through augury. Each took position on his respective hill and prepared a sacred space there. Remus claimed to have seen 6 birds, while Romulus said he saw 12 birds. Romulus asserted that he was the clear winner by 12 birds, but Remus argued that since he saw his 6 birds first, he had won.

2 Michael Parsons (1990) wrote about Sophocles's *Oedipus at Colonus* and Euripides's *Bacchae*, suggesting that Oedipus can be seen as an aspect of Theseus's own personality which he has split off and rejected and is similar to Dionysus and Pentheus. Here, the emphasis is on Theseus's authority as a ruler, forefather, and founder.

3 The translation is an adapted version of the translation by the Project Gutenberg, made by the author, adjusted for the comprehensibility of this text for an international readership.

4 [Goethe, Faust, Part I, Scene I: Freud quoted this in *Totem and Taboo* (1913), and once again in his *An Outline of Psycho-Analysis* (1940).]

References

Arendt, H. (1961). What is authority? In *Between past and future* (pp. 91–141). The Viking Press.

Barthes, R. (1979, January 7). Lecture in inauguration of the chair of literary semiology. *Collège de France.* (Original work published 1977, trans. Howard, Richard)

Bion, W.R. (1961). *Experiences in groups.* Tavistock Publications.

Boehlich, W. (Ed.). (1990). *The letters of Sigmund Freud to Eduard Slilberstein, 1871–1881.* Harvard University Press.

Chasseguet-Smirgel, J. (1985). The ego ideal and the psychology of groups. *Free Associations, 1C,* 31–60.

de Jouvenal, B. (1962). *On power.* Beacon Press.

Eisold, K. (1994). The intolerance of diversity in psychoanalytic institutes. *International Journal of Psychoanalysis, 75,* 785–800.

Eisold, K. (1997). Freud as leader: The early years of the Viennese society. *International Journal of Psychoanalysis, 78,* 87–104.

Ferenczi, S. (1910). Letter from Sándor Ferenczi to Sigmund Freud, April 5, 1910. In *The correspondence of Sigmund Freud and Sándor Ferenczi (1908–1914)* (Vol. 1, pp. 157–160).

Ferenczi, S. (1913). Letter from Sándor Ferenczi to Sigmund Freud, November 8, 1913. In *The correspondence of Sigmund Freud and Sándor Ferenczi (1908–1914)* (Vol. 1, p. 519).

Foucault, M. (1969). What is an author. In M. Foucault (Ed.), *Language, counter-memory, practice. Selected esseays and interwievs.* Cornell University Press.

Foucault, M. (1980). *Power/knowledge: Selected interviews and other writings 1972–1977.* Google Books: Colin Gordon.

Freud, S. (1913). *Totem and taboo: Some points of agreement between the mental lives of savages and neurotics (1913 [1912–13]). SE* (Vol. 13, pp. 7–162).

Freud, S. (1914). *On narcissism: An introduction. SE* (Vol. 14, pp. 67–102).

Freud, S. (1921). *Group psychology and the analysis of the ego. SE* (Vol. 18, pp. 65–144).

Freud, S. (1923). *The ego and the Id. SE* (Vol. 19, pp. 1–66).

Freud, S. (1924). *The dissolution of the oedipus complex. SE* (Vol. 14, pp. 171–180).

Freud, S. (1925). *An autobiographical study. SE* (Vol. 20, pp. 1–74).

Freud, S. (1926). *Inhibitions, symptoms and anxiety. SE* (Vol. 20, pp. 75–176).

Grosskurth, P. (1991). *The secret ring: Freud's inner circle and the politics of psychoanalysis.* Addison-Wesley.

Klein, M. (1932). The psycho-analysis of children. In *The international psycho-analytical library* (Vol. 22, pp. 1–379). The Hogarth Press.

Kojeve, A. (2014). *The notion of authority.* Verso.

Nunberg, H., & Federn, E. (1962). *Minutes of the Vienna psychoanalytic society (1906–1908)* (Vol. 1). International-University Press.

Parsons, M. (1990). Self-knowledge refused and accepted: A psychoanalytic perspective on the 'Bacchae' and the 'Oedipus at Colonus'. *Journal of Analytical Psychology, 35,* 19–40.

Parsons, T. (1991). *The social system.* Routledge. (Original work published 1951)

Paskauskas, R. A. (Ed.). (1993). *The complete correspondence of Sigmund Freud and Ernest Jones (1908–1939),* Introduction by Riccardo Steiner. Belknap Press.

Weber, M. (1968). *Economy and society: An outline of interpretative sociology* (Vol. 1). Bedminster Press.

Chapter 12

A Quick Look at Organisational Issues in European Psychoanalytic Institutions

Franziska Ylander

Trying to catch highlights of "organisational issues" in Europe is of course a challenge. I lean on my personal experiences and collected impressions from four years in the EPF Executive and then four years as elected European representative at the IPA Board. My function as "Eurorep" included keeping up close personal liaisons with six to seven EPF societies as their link to the IPA Board. Since eight years up to date, I have been part of the EPF Forum on Institutional Matters (IMF), where I have had the unique opportunity to take part in informative interviews on a group level with experienced members of more than a third of the European societies. This has offered a unique possibility to go deeply into what is my focus here – to underline *the impact of the psychoanalytic society* for the individual psychoanalyst, and to give some personal reflections on the differences between conflicts and levels of functioning in our psychoanalytical institutions.

The European region – the EPF – is composed of more than 40 societies. During the historic era of psychoanalysis – around 130 years – all countries except two (Sweden and Switzerland) have been involved in or exposed to active and destructive warfare.

During this era, many psychoanalytical societies have been born, but some have also died. Some societies have resurrected after wartime, and some even miraculously managed to survive, under strict observation or downright surveyance by political authorities. The stories about underground activities during warfare time and suffocating dictatorships are breathtaking, scary, and sometimes also funny.

In several cases, splitting of societies has been imminent, sometimes leading to hurtful and long-standing processes where splitting finally also happened. This has occurred in both old and new societies. The study of conflict themes, and whether these areas are recognizable and recurring in a way that might be specific for psychoanalytical organisations, has been in focus for the IMF work group.

On the other hand, there has not just been threats of splitting – during the last decade, we have, in Europe, experienced two cases of merging of established societies in two separate countries. In both cases, the process implied a merging of societies that had been born or created after the splitting of an "old" society many decades earlier. In both cases, the reunion/merging was made possible by long

DOI: 10.4324/9781032709819-18

processes of healing of old wounds and after implicit reparation of an original split. In both cases, an awareness of the necessity for a realistic and worked-through adaptation to changes in the surrounding world outside the psychoanalytical community probably made these fusions possible.

The "psychoanalytical community" manifests itself in several different institutional ways: in local societies; in federations of societies like EPF, Fepal, and APsaA; and of course, in the IPA, which is our common global membership organisation. IPA is most certainly an organisation, but membership in the IPA setting is individual, notwithstanding the fact that the membership of the individual analyst usually is connected to and administrated by a local society. One can also apply to be a "direct member" of the IPA if, for political or other reasons, it is not possible to join a local psychoanalytical IPA society.

My intention is to reflect on the primary importance *of the society* and to put emphasis on the relation between the individual psychoanalyst and his or her chosen organisation. I think most of our European membership would define, if not their "identity", then at least their "belonging" as "I am a member of the X Society".

The diversity of how organisational issues appear in Europe is apparent. This is understandable in many ways – there are huge differences in political traditions and cultural contexts between different countries located east, west, north, and south of the continent. Two training models – Eitingon and the French model – are coexisting among the more than 40 different societies within the regional federation EPF. Over 20 different languages are spoken within EPF. It is, in many ways, remarkable that these diversities seem to be contained within the concept of a more or less common *European identity*. I very much believe that this, too, is based on *joint tolerance and an enough amount of acceptance of existing differences*. This usually works fine in times of smooth functioning within the organisations, while in times of crisis, more fundamentalist tendencies and views about what is right or wrong can serve as a hotbed for conflicts.

It is worth mentioning a couple of recurring themes – issues that are recognizably similar in reports and narratives encountered in discussions with psychoanalysts engaged in the organisational activities of their different societies.

- Historically, many "old" societies have suffered problems concerning highly cathected matters on *heritage*, such as links and opposition related to the "founding fathers" of the society. It is obvious that today some "new" societies are involved in tackling the same conflict areas.
- Another area of huge impact for the functioning of many established societies is the struggle with what might be called "transgenerational problems". Who is going to – or will be allowed to – take over responsibilities in the organisation? Are the problems to find candidates for election to positions within a psychoanalytical society just connected to the workload, or are there more subtle and threatening obstacles? Administration and management rule the business of societies of today – matters of university relations, certification problems,

also health insurance dilemmas. The *psychoanalytical societies turn more and more into companies* that are running training organisation, protecting standards for certification, and supporting and organising outreach activities in the community.

- Many societies have ongoing internal, serious, and controversial discussions concerning *hierarchy and power*. The *training analyst function* has been questioned and even challenged in several Eitingon model societies, and the concepts of *training models* – including differences in settings and "in real life" application – are discussed. As stated earlier, many societies also report huge difficulties in finding members willing to take on responsibilities and the huge workloads of time necessary to safeguard high-quality training. Taking on responsibilities in a climate where decision-making might put you in a target position for projections and acting out of conflicts is risky. Well-trained and dedicated members seem to hesitate to take on responsibility, their commitment to psychoanalysis notwithstanding.

I want to emphasise that, during the last years, matters like these have, in some cases, led to quite alarming situations with destructive and splitting potential. It is our experience in the IMF – from our interviews with representatives from different EPF societies and between ourselves – that organisational matters are always relevant when looking at the history of the society and discussing the current everyday situation of the society in question. This is apparent in the report from the project EVP (Tuckett et al., 2020), an intervision project (without any formal affiliation to IPA or EPF) organised as a site visit program on a peer basis, focusing on the subject of training and of training organisation. This kind of workshops inevitably uncovers and activates organisational issues in the organisations studied, also far beyond the chosen focus subject.

It is of great importance for regional federations of societies like EPF, Fepal, and APsaA, and for umbrella organisations like IPA, to be aware of the institutional aspects of all important efforts to open discussions within and not least between psychoanalytical societies.

One cannot be but very touched by the high degree of devotion to the psychoanalytic project that is present among its members. I want to emphasize that the closest important psychoanalytic organisation is one's society. The society contains and implements the training and standards for training. It provides the stage for intense engagement in matters of power and competence. It is the base for how to be acknowledged in one's professional community in one's own country and within the regional and global psychoanalytical world.

The stability and stamina of one's society also provides the setting for how to survive economically as analyst, with huge differences in possibilities and conditions between countries and political systems. This is an important aspect of the context, which makes it comprehensible to understand some reactions, particularly European, in the wake of IPA's decision in 2017 to change minimal standards of the Eitingon model.

Like local societies, the regional federations, and the IPA Board are, indeed, psychoanalytical institutions – and highly charged psychoanalytical settings as well. Proceedings in these international settings tend to differ from how matters are run in local societies, being characterised by a persistent presence of something extremely multi-layered. So many different levels of looking at matters are constantly simultaneously under attention. In the dynamic communications in this kind of groups and organisations, it is possible to discern the constant influence of a more complicated way of looking at things. I believe it is a consequence of the rather specific process of formation we have all been going through in our personal analysis, in our training and supervision and through our clinical work. Regardless of our private and unique minds, and the outcome of our psychoanalytic experiences notwithstanding, we are all, by definition, forever victims of the activities of our UCS. After attending meetings in psychoanalytical administrative contexts and reflecting on my own contributions, not to speak of the fate of my sometimes-verbalised associations, I recognise in hindsight the traces of unconscious defensive work of mine as well as use and misuse of my psychoanalytical capacities.

My point with this short text is to address the important position of the individual analyst in relation to a specific kind of organisation, the local psychoanalytic society, a community that is part of one's everyday life. The analyst has been treated, trained, and followed closely by peers throughout his or her professional life. But the analyst as probably also an individual member in IPA, the global psychoanalytic organisation. In this kind of large organisation, intentions of best practice and openness towards the members unfortunately always risk being burdened by distance and by the political and unavoidable cultural aspects of difference.

I lean on my experiences from my society, my federation of societies, and from the experience of serving at the IPA Board as representative of my region. It is fascinating and intriguing how issues of organisational life in psychoanalytic institutions always express themselves through individuals – psychoanalysts – in ways that can be both helpful and destructive. A simple but, for me, uncontroversial conclusion is never to lose sight of the fact that issues of organisational life in psychoanalytic institutions, independent of size, always express themselves through individuals, but in a group setting, where it must be observed and understood on terms of the dynamics of the group.

Reference

Tuckett, D., Mehler, J. A., Collins, S., Diercks, M., Flynn, D., Frank, C., Millar, D., Skale, E., & Wagtmann, M. (2020). Psychoanalytic training in the Eitingon model and its controversies: A way forward. *International Journal of Psychoanalysis*, *101*, 1106–1135.

Chapter 13

History of the Protocol and the Principle of the French Model Training

Après-Coup and Overdetermination of Training Models

Bernard Chervet

Introduction

The expression "French model" refers both to the analytic method as practiced in France and to the French model of training to become a psychoanalyst.

The method used in France still refers to the classic standard treatment, with the fundamental rule highlighting the psychic functioning induced by it in each of the protagonists, the free association, and the evenly suspended attention. At the end of his life, Freud announced the rule consisting of two proposals: "Complete candor on one side and strict discretion on the other" (1940, p. 174).

This method is most efficient within a specific protocol: at least three sessions per week, couch-armchair setting, fixed duration of sessions of 45 minutes minimum, payment provided by the analysand, all in a "protected" space from the incentives emanating from sensory perception, to the benefit of the language enunciation of everything that comes to the analysand's mind, both verbal contents, affects, and body feelings.

The fundamental rule uses a paradox; it prescribes a freedom of expression that reveals a failure to express, but above all, a dimension "beyond" words is experienced through them. This beyond requires a specific psychic work carried out by the "après-coup" process, including a period of regression, like in the dreamwork.

Concerning the IPA's three official training models, there is currently a lot of discussion within the IPA about the training models resulting in some changes to the historical Eitingon model (1925). The decision to allow the number of sessions per week to vary from three to five triggered storms is the subject of considerable debates. As the enlargement was extended to three sessions, the French model was questioned and implicitly accused of having contaminated the historical model downwards. In fact, a much more general reflection could focus on their internal coherence and their flexibility of application and evolution.

However, we will focus on the French model without trying to compare it with Eitingon's model but rather question its foundations by recalling the historical and conflicting circumstances of its birth. It is the result of a double confrontational

DOI: 10.4324/9781032709819-19

conflict with the Eitingon model on the one hand and with other models used since then in Lacanian societies on the other hand. This conflict was at the centre of the splits of 1953 for the SPP, and 1964 for the birth of the APF.

Let us begin by reviewing a few historical points, then by recalling the criteria that constitute the French model with their concrete applications, and finally by making some theoretical reflections resulting from the consideration of the criteria supported by Lacan.

A Few Words of History

The practice of psychoanalysis was introduced in France in 1920 by Eugénie Sokolnicka. Freud's thinking was already known through various disciplines: medicine, arts, philosophy, etc. Then, it was Rudolph Loewenstein, trained at the Institute of Psychoanalysis in Berlin, who allowed the development of the young SPP founded in 1926.

Before the Second World War, the training model used by the SPP was the Berlin one promoted by Eitingon. After the war, the Paris Psychoanalytical Society, which was totally dispersed, reorganised. The rules concerning the practice of psychoanalysis were the same as those adopted before the war.

But a very pragmatic new parameter came into play: a strong demand for analysis and training. The post-war "baby boom", combined with the limited number of training analysts, concretely raised the question of the teaching of psychoanalysis and the training of new analysts, as well as that of the organisation of a training institute, with the choices that this implied between a certain number of options: independence or rapprochement with the university, practical modalities of the training course, etc. This high demand was at the origin of the practice of four sessions, and of the training psychoanalysis with three sessions per week, each of 45 minutes' duration. These criteria were extended to individual supervisions. And then, for the same reasons, the formula of collective supervisions was invented with the same principles. The main objective was to train a larger number of analysts in a much shorter period of time.

It was in this context that Lacan also promoted short sessions, to be distinguished from the introduction of his scansion technique. The framework of four sessions per week is gradually being accepted by the IPA, and the possibility of three sessions is tacitly accepted for personal psychoanalysis and supervised treatment.

Thus, the French model appeared first for pragmatic reasons and not for theoretical reasons. In the background, there was the disaster of war, the disappearance of the PP, and of course, the death of Freud, whose grief was masked by the torments of war. In 1953, under the aegis of Marie Bonaparte, the Paris Institute of Psychoanalysis was reopened. Major conflicts between Daniel Lagache and Sacha Nacht caused the 1953 split. This split was not the immediate consequence of the three sessions per week, nor that of the short sessions, nor of the scansion technique as practiced by Lacan. Daniel Lagache was a university professor who proposed a program close to the university models while, on the other hand, Sacha Nacht wanted an independent institute promoting another model that was considered too medical by his opponents but supported by Marie Bonaparte because it was more specifically psychoanalytic.

The official reasons for resignations and splits were therefore the training criteria with a war between several models, academic, medical, or centred on supervision. It is important to note that this is not a conflict between Eitingon's model and the French model.

This split led to the creation of the French Society of Psychoanalysis behind Daniel Lagache, who was quickly joined by Lacan and a small group of analysts from the SPP. It was then operated by Lacan and became Lacan's split with SPP and IPA. The dispute between models, which has been overshadowed, returns to the question of the variable duration of the sessions advocated by Lacan and by scansion, but not by the number of sessions.

In 1964, Jacques Lacan was dismissed from his position as a training analyst at the French Society of Psychoanalysis because of his scansion model. He left the SPP and created the École Freudienne de Paris (EFP), within which a model of validation of the quality of the analyst, named "the pass", would be developed. This second split led to the creation of the Association Psychanalytique de France (APF), which adopted the IPA's criteria for the practice and training.

In 1971, the APF abolished the training analysis and accepted the principle of testing all candidates regardless of their analyst.

The most essential point of this evolution was one of the two major criteria of the French model, the radical sealing between personal analysis and training. There is only one psychoanalysis, the personal analysis. This principle of sealing was extended in a nuanced way to the whole training. Rather, it is a limitation of interference between the different actors involved in the training.

At the same time, the reflection on training went on outside official societies and gave rise to the creation of the fourth group which theorised the "fourth analysis" related to supervision.

In 1994, the SPP abolished the obligation to follow a psychoanalysis with a "titulaire" (a full member with the functions of training analyst; a training member) in order to become a candidate. This is the "all couch" rule.

In 2004, when Daniel Widlöcher was President of the IPA, the minimum three sessions/week treatment model, used by the SPP and APF training institutes, was officially recognised by the IPA as a valid way to conduct an analysis and training.

Characteristics of the French Model: "Freedom" and the Separation of Functions

Let us leave aside the small differences existing between the SPP, the APF, the SPRF, and other societies (Belgium, Swiss, Quebec, etc.) using variants relating to the "French model". No complete French model has ever been described, except in terms of the criteria of "training analysis" and the training itself.

Two criteria are essential:

1. *Freedom*, a term which, by its double meaning, may have raised criticism of laxity. It is the dilemma between acquiring freedom through a long and tedious work of mentalisation or freeing oneself by discarding all that is unpleasant in order to escape this work. It is, in fact, the freedom of "free" association, the freedom to develop the identification process with the way of thinking required to be an analyst in sessions, which implies different conceptions of an ideal psychic functioning targeted by the standard treatment.
2. *Separation of functions.* Absolute watertightness between personal analysis and training, and limitation of interference between those responsible for training.

Freedom

- Freedom in the choice of the analyst. Currently, the patient can undertake a psychoanalysis with any IPA psychoanalyst (SPP) or with an analyst of any obedience (APF) without the need for this analyst to be a training member.
- Freedom for the analyst to decide whether three or four sessions per week are more appropriate, and also to accept or refuse a particular patient.
- Freedom for the institution to accept or refuse the candidate (freedom of selection criteria, based, in fact, on this identification with a regressive way of thinking, sensitive to the unconscious).
- Freedom for institutes to organise their training programs, seminars, working groups, and individual and collective supervisions.
- Freedom concerning the moment when a candidate can request their entry into a training institute in order to start their training.
- Freedom in the choice of supervisors.
- Freedom in the choice of seminars, working groups, days, colloquia, congresses that candidates have to follow.

Of course, this freedom does not mean no incentive – quite the contrary – but incentive calls on the candidate's sense of responsibility and desire to learn, their curiosity, and the personal journey involved in their choices.

Sealing and Interference Limitation

This freedom goes hand in hand with the fact that the personal analyst does not interfere in any way, at any time, in the training process. Psychoanalysis as individual treatment is clearly distinct and separate from training that supports the desire to become an analyst, a desire that can contain multiple latent meanings involving various unconscious desires evoked in session.

This has consequences: an ethics of discretion is required on the part of the candidate's analyst and also extends to training, in particular to supervisions, which, through countertransference, engages the candidate's personal analysis, past or present. Such limitation of interferences tries to prevent against a group mentality.

It is worth highlighting here how the French model evolved specifically. Several years of personal analysis are required (at least three) before starting the training. A few years ago, candidates were implicitly expected to attend the training after completing their personal analysis and having a private practice. Currently, personal analysis often continues while training is underway, which allows for associations on the training as session material. This is not simple but is preferable to insulation. From this point of view, the French model and the Eitingon model maintain points of contact, the separation of functions being increasingly respected by the institutes that have adopted the Eitingon model, since the abolition of "reporting". Nevertheless, in the Eitingon model, personal analysis, a very scheduled training, and supervision remain interdependent.

Here is an example: the concrete organisation of the French model in the SPP's institutes (schematic presentation).

1. Request to open a file (application) to become an "analyst in training" (a "candidate" in other countries).
2. If the institute's response is positive, appoint three training analysts (commissioners) to conduct three preliminary interviews.
3. The three interviews with the three commissioners.
4. Presentation of the three interviews to the training commission (about six to ten trainers) > admission/refusal/adjournment.
5. Authorisation to start supervisions and incentives to attend training seminars, congresses, etc.
   Possible option (specially supervised training): request to wait one year to start the second supervision with or without indication of first individual or collective supervision. In the case of the especially supervised training, the first supervisor comes to present the year of supervision to the training commission, which may or may not give its agreement for the second.
6. Request for the end of the course after agreement of the two supervisors, with a record of all seminars, colloquia, and other activities during the training.
7. Interview with a coordinator to speak about the training, supervisions, seminars, and specific activities, as well as about some possible difficulties encountered and feedback reflections about training period.
8. End of training within the end of training commission, which brings together two different commissions (12 to 18 training members), with the two supervisors, admission commissioners, and directors of the seminars attended: validation/nonvalidation with request to continue the training (third supervision, for example, or continuation of one of them) or end of the training.

Metapsychological Point of View

To approach our theoretical reflection, we will consider some correlations between models and psychological functioning:

1. From the point of view of the transference of authority and the idealising transference active in analysis and training, the correlations with childhood and its reminiscences are obvious. Each model inherits and stimulates memories about school, learning, knowledge, authority, and so on.
2. From the point of view of training and transmission, there is not a single model of teaching that is fully satisfactory, hence the desire to invent new ones, neglecting the importance of the identification involved in transmission and its reference to heritage and mourning.
3. From the point of view of treatment success, no model can guarantee the success of analytical treatment, hence the hope that a change of model will overcome resistance.
4. From the point of view of the adaptation between the models and psychic functioning, according to their psychic organisation, a model can be better used by this or that patient and candidate. Each model is driven by the desire to offer the patient the *Nebenmensch*, the *fellow human being*, the person who is well informed, the person who has the right answer, the good-enough mother, the father as a support of tender authority, allowing him to resume his psychological development. For some, the protocol with three sessions per week is in phase with neurotic patients; the one with more sessions per week is supposed to be better adapted to borderline organisations, while for others fewer sessions are then preferable, to cope with massive narcissistic and psychotic transferences.
5. From a theoretical point of view, two points:
   - It is the relationship to continuity-discontinuity that embodies the reflections resulting from the confrontation of the French and Eitingon models.
   - The question of temporality and superego dominates the debates in France, with the passage from traumatic atemporality to the timelessness of the dynamic unconscious and to temporality marked by the renunciation engaged in the Oedipal mourning that establishes the superego.

In both cases, the reflection is back to the après-coup process.

Continuity-Discontinuity

Psychoanalytical work must promote the efficiency of psychic operations required in the presence and absence of the analyst. With their three or four or five sessions per week, all the training models place the effects of the couple continuity-discontinuity at the very centre of the technique.

The French model would be expected to better respect the psychic discontinuity due to absence and better elicit a two-stage psychic functioning based on the specific dynamics of the après-coup, with its latency period between the two times.

The Anglo-Saxon model of five sessions per week would be expected to promote continuity that would protect the patient from the trauma of discontinuity.

Such a demarcation, based on a clear reality, between the models and the couple continuity-discontinuity, does not seem to be sustainable from a metapsychological point of view. However, an official recognition of the après-coup in French psychoanalysis, and its virtual absence in the Anglo-Saxon one, reflects the analyst's different conceptions and listening to the session material. For some, it is understood as the traumatic "shock" expression of the compulsion of repetition, for others as the result of the après-coup process. If continuity is the desired and idealised goal, the après-coup effect will not be recognised; on the contrary, if discontinuity is privileged, the necessity for an illusion of continuity will be neglected.

We find overdetermination by the latent theoretical foundations involved in the analyst's listening, his or her conception of an ideal mental functioning. These theoretical conceptions seem to be the main benchmark for differentiation; however, we must keep in mind that the analyst's mental functioning prevails over his or her implicit and explicit theories.

Temporality

Thus, the question of temporality is targeted by Lacan's contributions and gives them their relevance. While the context of reducing session time and the number of sessions for pragmatic reasons discussed earlier may have encouraged this call to make the duration and number of sessions fluctuate, it should be noted that this is always in the direction of a reduction.

On the metapsychological level, we can consider that Lacan's proposals seek a solution to a clinical aspect faced by any analyst, the regressive attraction involved in the repetition compulsion to which responds the painful working through (*Durcharbeitung*).

Lacan saw that regression and recollection can get bogged down in the compulsion of repetition. It was probably this painful aspect for the analyst, which made him break the common rules, by introducing the reduction of session time and "scansion", that is, a degree of violence having the value of an interpretative attempt by a traumatic act. This traumatic impact bears the hope of triggering within the session the processes engaged in libidinal co-excitation, and thus to generate an emergence of desire.

This proposal is obviously to be discussed with Lacanian colleagues who are keen to think about their practice.

For us, "scansion" is an invitation to think about the interpretation. It must be (contained) in the interpretation. The asymmetry comes from this psychic act, not from the "Prince's will". The interpretation must take into account the value of the scansion, to the benefit of the timelessness and timeliness of the couple. We grant to regression the hope of letting the feelings of lack appear, and we dedicate to interpretation the ability to free the psychic operations that respond to them. The challenge of our work, a challenge that is never certain, is to awaken the imperatives of mentalisation. Before stopping for debate, it should also be pointed out that changes in models generally are going in one and only way of a reduction in the number of sessions, the duration of the sessions, the duration of the analysis, etc. It started with Otto Rank and the "birth trauma" and gave rise to important comments from Freud. Beyond the legitimacy of this concern, this reductive tendency and the passion that accompanies it are presented as a clinical element. This tendency to decrease can be seen as an effect of the tendency to free oneself from the psychological work required by the presence–absence oscillation acted upon by the sessions, an oscillation that calls to mind the reminiscences of the presence–absence oscillation of the parents and, therefore, of the primary scene. It is a question of eliminating the endo-perceptions of lack by creating a materialised lack, a lack of session time, instead of the much more elusive one that reflects the powerlessness of the psyche to eliminate the traumatic dimension. A new discussion arises on the conceptions of an ideal psychic functioning, active in the analyst's countertransference: Is analysis in the service of the construction of feelings of continuity or the recognition of a fundamental discontinuity internal to the psyche? Finally, on a pragmatic level, it should be noted that such a desire to reduce the duration of the analysis, the number of sessions, and the duration of the sessions goes against the comfort required for the analyst's mental work. When defending these decreases, the analyst works against himself, but especially against the analysis, by depriving himself of this minimum of comfort. A countertransference phobia of the analytical situation is evident here.

Reference

Freud, S. (1940). *An outline of psychoanalysis. SE* (Vol. 23, pp. 139–208). (Original work published 1938)

Part VI

The Vicissitudes and Maternal Function of Psychoanalytic Organisations

Chapter 14

The Maternal Function of Psychoanalytical Organisations

Jasminka Šuljagić

"Great is Diana of the Ephesians" is the title of a short text written by S. Freud in 1911, 100 years after the publication of the poem with the same title by J. S. Goethe.

This shouting of praise for the goddess, "Great is Diana of the Ephesians," was a collective cry expressed on the verge of her abolition, Diana being lost, only to be found later in a new mother-goddess with the coming of Christianity.

In a few lines, Freud tells us the story of the continuity of this transmission at a site in Ephesus whose foundation dates back legendarily to the Amazons, from the cult of an ancient mother-goddess Oupis, via the Greek Artemis, to the Roman Diana, and finally to the Holy Virgin Mary. Wild goddesses, worshiped during orgiastic rites, were transformed into a goddess of chastity, a pure mother, the Mother of God.

One century before Freud's text, with the same title, Goethe had written about the requirement to renounce replicated material forms, in favour of searching for them only "behind Man's foolish forehead, in his mind"; he also described a craftsman who, upon hearing "a raging crowd. . . with skill and patience" (cited in Carus, 1907), remained persistent in his work.

In the same year as he published "Great Is Diana of the Ephesians", Freud read the "Postscript" to the Schreber case at a Weimar IPA congress, initiating the theme of "totemic habits of thought", which was continued in his *Totem and Taboo*. However, the theme of the maternal goddess did not find its significant place here, nor did it 27 years later, in *Moses and Monotheism*. Mostly in margins, in notes, or very concisely, Freud told us about an organisation

Figure 14.1 Diana of the Ephesians.

Source: From an illustration by H. Knackfuss in Diintzer's German edition of *Goethe's Works*.

DOI: 10.4324/9781032709819-21

marked by "institutions of maternal law", the period of "Great Mothers" after the murder of the father of the primal horde and before the patriarchal family order was set up. Afterward, with the re-establishment of a patriarchal order, mother goddesses appeared as compensation for the slight upon mothers.

From these points, several threads were echoed in later theories:

- "Censorship of the lover," by M. Fain, D. Braunschweig. The maternal function implies a complex reversal of investment, turning away from the infant to her female desire, which, for the infant, opens a path towards sleep, dreamwork, and double identification.
- The maternal as unknown, unrecognised, "like a shadow", unapproachable, the renunciation of the mother both in human development and in the genesis of religion.
- Mother as an object of transmission, transformation, continuity, and discontinuity.
- Representation of the "maternal" as de-sexualised, disembodied, virginal, saturated with idealised images, fearing her vulnerability.
- Repudiation of femininity in both sexes as a repudiation of the child's position of helplessness (Hilflosigkeit) in relation to the mother.
- "Now Dr. B's child is coming!" At this moment, he held in his hand the key that would have opened the "'doors to the Mothers', but he let it drop" (Freud about Breuer and Anna O, 1932).

Afterwards, Berta Papenhaim became a founder of Jewish feminism in Germany, and we have inaugurated theories about the seductive mother, dead mother, absent mother, containing mother, and good-enough mother.

Approaching our theme about transpositions and fantasies of the maternal function in analytical organisations, we are in the position to investigate slightly whether we can use psychoanalytic theory and our concepts to understand the life of our organisations, and whether these organisations owe their peculiarity to the fact that they consist of members who have been going through their own analyses, considering transference remnants and the proximity of transference regression.

I will choose two main axes for closer consideration, with their constantly interchanging perspectives and levels.

The Maternal as an Unknown Source

"Sometimes I could visualize the situation, unfolding in the analysis, as one in which the patient was a foetus to whom the mother's emotions were communicated but to whom the stimulus for the emotions, and their source was unknown" was written by Bion in 1962. Does this concern our theme, the passive expectation of care which is impersonal, as done by itself, the silent and unpaid fulfilment of tasks for institutions of tasks for institutions, collusion in maintaining and transmitting the secrecy and wealth of the maternal?

It is beyond the scope of this presentation to examine in detail the concept of passivity, whether in the analytic process or in development, from Freud's remark about the struggle against passivity (with very specific meaning), which "give[s] the analyst an unusual amount of trouble" (1937), to the later developed concept of "passivisation", a position of receptivity in relation to the mother's care, as a crucial requirement of the analytical process.

However, it might be worthwhile to further reflect on and research whether allowing the establishment of an organisation of passivity during one's own analysis, and the analyst's task of promoting the regressive work of passivity during the analytical process, is interrelated with the transposition of these to a position within the institution, whether this is a peculiarity of the institutional life of psychoanalytical organisations? The passivity of members of our organisations is remarkable and often discussed; in every society, there are around one-quarter to one-third of members who are involved and interested in the activity of any society they belong to.

"*Note the difference* between the leader who is to show the *way* to thinking, and the 'mother' on whom the psyche is to be allowed to be parasitic-projective identification, psychotic dependence", Bion said (1992/1982).

Thinking about what is very early on designated as a "specific action": the place of the mother in the origin and early structuring of the psyche; the constitutive, founding dimension later called the holding capacity; reverie; the primal mother preoccupation; the containing function. All this remains under the veil of the unknown, obscured by the mysterious lap of transformation from "me" to "another", from "being" ("the breast") to "having". The first passivity is dependence on an object that is alluring, ambiguous, seductive, and strange, the other. From all variations and moves in transference, we know about the overlapping of these functions with the function of an analyst, and further transposed, where the unknown might be replaced by the unrecognised, with denial of both hate and work necessarily done, or avoided through idealisation. It could even take the form of worship of the figure of a "purified" and glorious mother, often the mother of origin, a charismatic leader on one hand; on the other, terrifying maternal representations, leading to destructiveness.

Through the note on idealisation, we are going towards the second axis, "of turning the mother into an untouched virgin" (Freud, 1918), with all the background of sensuality of mothers, and of the "taboo of woman".

A Conflict Between Maternal Function and Oedipal Structuring

The narrative about the period of "great mothers" after the murder of the father of the primal horde might reflect these conflicting realities of woman and mother, "from a utopian perspective", alternating in days and nights, constituting them at the beginning of life. When they are fixed in a lasting, apparently still and smooth manner, this could reveal a form of narcissistic retreat of the maternal, excluding paternity by elimination of the primal scene.

This maternal transmission is visible in paintings of Leonardo da Vinci referred to by Freud, the representation of a virgin mother in a fused relationship with her own mother and child, deprived of the paternal presence, also as the totem's child, and deified, the idealised link of Virgin with the child.

This might remind us of representations of dyad transmissions in our institutions, where not only is the third external party mostly avoided (a reluctance to engage professionals), but the organisation itself also becomes the disturbing third, with a sharp division between highly valued "scientific" and devalued "organisational" tasks. The latter are accordingly avoided and seen to be repetitive, purely mechanical and operational activities, leading only to exhaustion; or as if these just happen "there", done by "someone else", almost in secrecy, and surely "only for power". Exaggerated, this takes the form of a strict organisational approach, claiming that the life of our organisations has nothing to do with its psychoanalyst members, or with our theories in an attempt at comprehension.

"It is frightening when mothers become shaky; they stand between us and our demise", Freud told us (Freud, 1899). The emerging vulnerability and void are instantaneously covered by an abundance of representations of phallic power, and nearby, there is also a place for fetishes to appear, the danger of what might appear as an iconoclastic approach, not quite unknown to us. Sometimes, it is hard to distinguish it from the investigation of all the plenitude of forms and formations, quite various, not only visible, and conflictual in their meanings.

It could be surprising to learn, following representations of the mother-goddesses of Freud's short text "Great Is Diana of the Ephesians", in their mythological attributes, cults, and mysteries, that the many layers of breasts on the pectoral of Diana of the Ephesians may not be breasts at all; that Greek Artemis is not a mother at all but a huntress, a goddess of transition, remaining eternal at the threshold of sexual maturity, only becoming the goddess of childbirth from the 5th century. She was virginal, free, radiant, with a wild and shining nature, but also known for the bloodiest rites, with a multitude of sacrifices. Her predecessor, Oupis (Anatolian Kybele, Great Goddess of the Mountains and Animals, Mother of Gods) was worshipped by priests who, immersed in orgiastic frenzies, ritually castrated themselves and then dressed themselves in women's clothing; the same applied to Attis, her son and lover, prevented by her from moving apart and growing up, but after he had fertilised the earth (the mother) with his blood, he was continually being resurrected anew, as a boy (Budin, 2016; Gasparro, 1985; Rogers, 2012).

Figure 14.2 Statue of Artemis of Ephesus in the Vatican Museum.

This might now bring us towards many questions about psychoanalytic training, and to the necessity of forming missing representations for the work (both "maternal" and "paternal") of our institutional life, or of reviving oscillations between many of its forms and meanings. The work of the maternal, in transmissions and transformations, *marked by intrinsic internal conflict*, could show us the traces. This concerns psychic elaboration in a broad sense, a preconscious work allowing identification with the third, absent or unknown which our organisations are for us.

"If I published some similar writing in praise of the great Artemis . . . , I should have written on the reverse of the title page, 'No one can become acquainted with what he does not love'" (Goethe, in the letter to Jacobi, 10 March 1812).

Figure 14.3 Dianna of Versailles, 1st century.

Shortly, About Training

The important theme about two complementary perspectives of training, "for the individual" and "for the organisation", appeared during the Colloquium on Training, in London, 1995, and continued a bit in the EPF Bulletin the next year. The raised issue is that candidates will become members of the organisation, with the task of transmitting psychoanalysis, and that "analytic training was not just a *dyadic phenomenon*" but also concerns the "institutional third."

A keynote paper was titled "A Question of Balance", and discussion was moved in accordance with different training systems: In which way is this understood and dealt with, that is, whether and how do we think about this during selection, admission, and the organisation of training (Daniel, 1996; Erlich, 1996).

An always-present dilemma relates to imposing on, intruding into, or interfering with (on the one hand) or to "infantilisation", allowing transference regression (on the other). Whether candidates are deprived of learning organisational structure and tasks or pushed towards them too early is also a question about the protective shield of the maternal.

The maternal, as an origin and its various functions, is what promotes growth and differentiation, but it is also the carrier of a regressive pull towards the undifferentiated.

Are solutions in pragmatic, concrete forms, with an "education-pure" characteristic, making them known and acknowledged, or might they appear in a different way, which could allow psychic elaboration and internal work, and which would be more for members than for candidates?

References

Bion, W. R. (1962). *Learning from experience*. Karnac Books.

Bion, W.R. (1992). *Cogitations*. Karnac Books. (Original work published 1982)

Budin, S. (2016). *Artemis*. Routledge.

Carus, P. (1907). Goethe's polytheism and christianity. Illustrated. *The Open Court, 1907*(7), Article 6.

Daniel, P. (1996). A question of balance. *Psychoanalysis in Europe, EPF Bulletin, 47.*

Erlich, S. (1996). Discussion of Patricia Daniel's paper. *Psychoanalysis in Europe, EPF Bulletin, 47.*

Freud, S. (1899). Letter from Freud to Fliess, July 3, 1899. In *The complete letters of Sigmund Freud to Wilhelm Fliess (1887–1904)* (Vol. 42, pp. 358–359).

Freud, S. (1911). *Great is Diana of the Ephesians. SE* (Vol. 12, pp. 342–344).

Freud, S. (1918). *The Taboo of virginity (contributions to the psychology of love III). SE* (Vol. 11, pp. 191–208).

Freud, S. (1932). Letter from Sigmund Freud to Stefan Zweig, June 2, 1932. In *Letters of Sigmund Freud (1873–1939)* (Vol. 51, pp. 412–413).

Freud, S. (1937). *Analysis terminable and interminable. SE* (Vol. 23, pp. 209–254).

Freud, S. (1939). *Moses and monotheism: Three essays. SE* (Vol. 23, pp. 1–138).

Gasparro, G. S. (1985). *Soteriology and mystic aspects in the cult of cybele and attis*. E. J. Brill.

Rogers, G. M. (2012). *The mysteries of artemis of ephesus*. Yale University Press.

Chapter 15

About the Vicissitudes of New Societies

Gábor Szőnyi

Early Development of Our Psychoanalytic Organisations

When and How Does the Life of an Analytic Organisation Begin?

A professional wants to become an analyst for his own sake, while the International Psychoanalytical Association (IPA) wants to have organisations which are capable of maintaining the growth of psychoanalysis through newer and newer generations. New groups are born in this conflict field.

A professional becomes an analyst for his own sake. However, at the end of training, he finds himself being a member of an analytic organisation. An analyst works alone. Therefore, he cannot maintain his professional competence and attitude in loneliness, as a hermit. He needs exchange, a network, which contains. He longs to be part of the analytic world and gets disappointed when he becomes a member just of a professional society with similar problems any other such organisation is coping with.

Colleagues choose analytic training for personal goals. In a country where no analytic organisation exists, the new analysts face the requirement to form a study group and its further steps together with others. Although most of them are familiar with different psychotherapeutic organisations, the psychoanalytic ones are uncanny and often mystic, and there are inherent difficulties, such as:

> *You join only individually and often leave/separate from your original professional psychotherapy group where you used to feel at home. The respect one has gained during one's professional career vanishes to a great extent, until it will be replaced by developing analytic competence and identity.*
>
> *Although IPA gives external support to the development of new organisations (site visit, sponsoring committee, liaison committee), unavoidably, it infantilises. The new groups are born with lots of conflicts.*

Unavoidably, there is a natural conflict field both for the individual and the organisation. If my formation to becoming an analyst falls together with the formation of

DOI: 10.4324/9781032709819-22

a new analytic group, the situation gets much more complex and vulnerable, while my capability to look out from my individual perspective is very narrow, and the containing capacity of the organisation in formation is very week.

In a survey we made in Europe a couple of years ago (Szőnyi et al., 2017), we found that the idealisation (and counter-idealisation) of the personal analyst and psychoanalysis per se gets transferred also onto the analytic society. Consequently, disillusion with the organisation will be of same high quantity and quality.

I am going to focus on how historical and repetitive are connected in the current stand of affairs, and on some developmental characteristics of new analytic organisations.

According to the IPA Institutional Task Force's report, fears come "primarily from two related and overlapping areas: training and intergenerational relationships".[1]

How Come New Analytic Groups to Earth?

Traditionally, new groups are born:

- Through splitting off from an existing society
- Due to internal conflicts
- Having been hosted (in a "mother" society)
- On the charismatic initiative (follower collection) of key figures

The IPA-ING (International New Groups Committee) drops in when a group submits an application for study group status, while the EPI/PIEE (European Psychoanalytic Institute, earlier Psychoanalytic Institute for Eastern Europe)[2] takes care from the beginning. Therefore, it faces the combination of birth "due to charismatic initiative" and splitting off from the institute.

Organisational-Developmental Phases

The way from the first local IPA direct member until becoming a still small but established and self-confident society is quite long. The formation of new psychoanalytic societies is a long process, often accompanied by traumatic events. From the IPA-ING perspective, it is worth differentiating the following phases:

- Pre-application phase ("pregnancy") pre-study group (6–20 years)
- Application ("birth") transition into a study group (1–5 years)
- Study group ("infancy") (6–20 years)
- Provisional society ("adolescence") (4–8 years)
- New/young component society; integration amongst the "old" IPA/EPI societies (5–10 years)

Which makes **20–30 years** or **more**. This covers two to four analytic generations. Development goes on in the interplay of (internal and external) cohesive and destructive forces.

Repetition of Early Conflict Patterns and the Capacity to Split

Basic feelings of young groups/societies are weakness and inferiority toward the broader community of analytic organisations. Psychoanalytic training provides you with a "psychoanalytic genealogy" – to be analysed by someone who was analysed by someone who was analysed by someone – back to the first fathers/mothers. A typical conflict originates from the "competition of roots": the founding members of a new society are trained and socialized in and by (members from) different elder societies, and the leading figures fight on who of them represents "the true analytic tradition".

Usually, the members of the first generation are in collegial and private relationships or have even family ties with each other. Those "shadow" relations define also the positions in the professional field. However, when becoming members of the study group, the positions may change profoundly – the respected people turn into students in relation to the representatives of the analytical world. The reorganisation of the – relative – status liberates creative energies but also reinforces covered conflicts and competitions. In the EE groups, those stressful relations might have been redoubled by knowledge about unacceptable roles and actions of some colleagues, committed during the communistic era, and which would contradict the democratic-ethical solidity, prerequisite of analytic functioning and teaching. It is important to notice that such constellations can be found also in the histories of elder societies, especially during their reorganisation after WW2. All this makes difficult to accept each other in the group. People feel forced for working together by an external power – IPA: "It is not decent to be judged by your peers and friends."

The fact is that the first generation is overloaded with roles and tasks, being in many respects junior and senior simultaneously; the tension who is in power which allows defining and doing things. Reading the histories of analytic societies, we find disruptions of some kind at the beginning. Most societies have started the same way – with one or two "great leading persons". This helps the foundation and becomes often the origin of later difficulties. The transmission of leadership from the first generation is often very painful, and traumatic.

Surprising how little is written and transferred about the pre-history in EE developing groups. It repeats the culture of "being in underground", the secrecy, and the unspoken knowledge. Auto-aggressive or regressive reactions within the society show up easily when members feel too helpless in the world outside.

The society as a place for freedom of thought and freedom of discussion needs protection. Organisational fears lead to avoiding the real tough arguments, to evade internal conflicts. Disagreeing implies not just a break of loyalty but even betrayal.

Psychoanalytic interpretations and diagnosing of each other often do not help, especially not during a fight, but become an organisational resistance against open discussion of painful questions.

The *early life* of a psychoanalytic society starts from one to three persons who gained analytic training somehow, somewhere – in/by the help of an already-existing IPA component society. In EE also from the EPI.

As mentioned, those persons had been trained usually at different places. Notwithstanding, they are locally outstanding figures, each other's supporters, or rivals in the scene. They already have prestige and followers. They have history, and several types of shadow relationships – being in the same social and professional network of the local community – which, unavoidably, will influence, mostly undiscussed and unconsciously the forming internal structure of the group.

That is normal in such an organisation, while its consequences easily appear as personal-interpersonal difficulties and which cause destructive group development. Organisation sign/symptom is, for example, an evolving conflict about who represents the "true" psychoanalysis who can say what is "true psychoanalytic". You also might have met with the annihilating remark to a candidate at your group's case discussions: "what you say/what you do is not psychoanalytic." (The hidden message: you do not belong among us.) You may blame the actors, but it can be perceived, simultaneously, as an organisational defence, because making open the background conflicts threatens the group's survival – this way, the possibility to become an IPA study group/society.

In the seventieth, when I started my training in Hungary, we were in an ex lex status from the point of IPA: the old society (founded in 1913) had been dissolved by the communistic state in 1949. There were a handful of analysts who turned into direct members of IPA, this way without being members of a containing society. In the middle seventieth, negotiations for the Hungarian group's reintegration went on, and the supervisions I already fulfilled as a non-public candidate of a non-public study group (the cause: in the Soviet imperium, you were not permitted to form civil organisations). Our analytic group went through all stages – study group, provisional society, and component society. The story ended parallel with the fall of the Soviet Union. Anyhow, I was passionately involved into the development of and battling inside our society. I attributed most problems to the personality of the actors, especially to those holding offices, although my group analytic practice helped to understand some events in other terms as well. But I must confess that only having served long time in EPI and ING, plus the experiences in sponsoring and liaison committees convinced me retrospectively, that what I lived through in my developing society had been most part typical troubles and pains of growing. The work and discussions in the EPF society forum added a further historical viewpoint: early developmental constellations and trauma often appear repetitively in later phases of the organisation (so what?).

The Position of the Candidates

Splits and crises in analytic organisations are connected to training, without exception. This underlines the importance to review the organisational position of the new generation – the candidates and the society.

In the last decades, the role of becoming analysts seems to undergo seminal changes in most societies, characterised mainly by more autonomy in the student's role, higher respect by the already members and more ways of integration into the life of the society. More or less, this questions the hierarchical structure but does not really rock the genealogical relations which permeate the analytic community. Normally, it goes together with urges to revise the training system. Internally, in many societies, the reduction of new candidates represents a threat; externally, the high demand for analysts *and analytic candidates* to teach analytic(ally oriented) psychotherapy influences the debates on training.

In new groups, the first generations *in local training* are in a special situation. They have teachers who are, in many other ways, too close to them, whom they must accept and whom they often do not respect. *They are on whom the new trainers learn to train.* Their trainers had the opportunity/burden to obtain training abroad – which they are pressed to give up. Unavoidably, they are involved into the turbulences of the formation period. The privacy of personal analysis and supervision sometimes cannot be safeguarded on the desirable level, and the organisation cannot provide the holding which an established society can. Complaint on lack of feeling at home in the society is frequent and might become pre-runner of the split "analysts are good, the society is bad".

Is it reasonable to discuss where our societies are in light of our own history today? And to assess the other way round: *Has an organisation the capacity to split?*

The Otherness of New Societies in EE

Explosion of Psychoanalysis in EE

After the fall of the Soviet Empire, psychoanalysis appeared in all EE countries. There had been started a "run for help and run to help": individuals, groupings, and analytic organisations provided several (divergent) options, without any interconnections but the claim for IPA recognition of the offered training. The extent and pressure of that development were far beyond the capacities and coping tools of IPA-ING, and of the IPA-EPF joint EE committees.[3] Since 1989, around 15–20 groups became component societies or are on the way of becoming, and over 300 new analysts are from the region.

Special Features of PIEE/EPI

The PIEE-EPI was an institute without previous models:

- It was founded in a co-operation between IPA and EPF.
- It had no seat, no office, but a board and staff of analysts from different countries who met during schools and sometimes on weekend retreats.

- Personal analysis and supervision were provided by training analysts from different countries, often in shuttle or condensed settings.
- Evaluations were carried out with inclusion of external teachers.
- The trainees of the institute had to form themselves into new IPA study groups.
- The institute was limited to that work and had an ending.

The PIEE/EPI was an incubator for becoming groups. It organised the whole process from getting in touch with psychoanalysis until qualification and beyond. In the given situation – a bunch of initiatives, an unexpected high demand on analytic training and on founding new, internationally recognised national analytic organisations – the institute faced the following tasks:

- Consolidation of the different training initiatives
- Initial evaluations for training, which also includes:

  - The *feasibility* of the whole training *as a project*
  - The actual stand of the developing local pre-study group
  - Individual mentoring
  - Site visits of board members when study group application gets close

Looking back, it was absolutely understandable but took the institute's board by surprise: we had to manage/mentor the transmission from the "home" EPI into a study group under the authority of the ING, a "fearful" agency. It turned out that there were groupings which did want, but also which did not, want to be born.

Some morals from witnessing those pains: do not run and force application. It is better to reach first a level which goes above IPA requirements. And the opposite: not to wait too long with application (if the group's development stagnates, press the group to progress). In case of stagnation, look for (hidden) unsolvable internal conflicts. Accept that there are situations where the "held all local applicants together" does not work. Understand that becoming a study group means to leave the institute where all of them were trained, contained, and had lots of colleagues.

In a broader view, we had to take into consideration the general processes and issues encountered in group/institutional formation in EE in the last 30 years, due to the social-political earthquake, the dissolution of the Soviet Empire. That means we needed to add to the analytic and group view the systemic/unconscious organisational view to achieve good-enough understanding. The PIEE/EPI met those challenges, good and bad, in which the IPA-EPF cooperation played an important role.

In EPI, we experienced several times that colleagues from the same location were on very good terms at the schools but wrestled with extreme difficulties when they faced: it is time to transform into a formal analytic organisation at home; they tried to stay under the umbrella of EPI, although it was clear to everybody that it means getting stuck in the pre-study group phase. In my view, a major reason is that EPI functions as a container, both vertically – having international teachers and being in a subsystem of IPA-EPF cooperation – and horizontally – being together with a big number of candidates and analysts who are in similar situation, which reduces and dilutes the interpersonal problems brought from home. And application for study group status means leaving the container EPI.

Organisational anxieties and *organisational* defences are an inherent part also of analytic societies. To their understanding, we need more than understanding individuals and groups.

The permanent discussion on the "crisis of psychoanalysis" is an important topic but, in my experience, taught PIEE/EPI to take as much care for shaping groups as for the training of the individuals.

After the fall of the Soviet Empire, psychoanalysis appeared in all EE countries (Kutter, 1992). As I pointed our earlier, a professional becomes an analyst for his own sake. However, at the end of training, he finds himself being a member of an analytic organisation. An analyst works alone. Therefore, he cannot maintain his professional competence and attitude in loneliness, as a hermit. He needs exchange, a network, which contains. He longs to be part of the analytic world and gets disappointed when he becomes a member just of a professional society with similar problems any other such organisation is coping with (Gabbard & Ogden, 2009; Junkers et al., 2008). If you meet papers written by analysts on the functioning of analytic societies, the majority is quite ruthlessly critical about their way of being and describes what goes on in individual terminology, sometimes in individual psychopathology. I very much know how extremely difficult it is to look at the problems and crisis also from a group dynamical point of view. Especially difficult is to see distractive events as organisational symptoms and distractive processes as organisational defences (see for instance, Stokoe, 2011).

It was also the institute's task to make the transition as smooth as possible – and to collaborate with IPA-ING in that process. Before forming a study group, PIEE served as a holding environment, more than the support of IPA sponsoring committees can give. Not surprisingly, the transition from PIEE to IPA study group (which means leaving PIEE and standing on their own foot) went on with many difficulties, especially of the feeling of getting lost. The sponsoring committee, delegated by IPA ING (International New Groups Committee) meant not only new people but also a new type of relationship between the local group and the "international people" (and IPA), although ING tried to reduce the tension by inviting also PIEE teachers into those committees.

Quite often, there was the danger of splitting up before the start. To prevent such development, PIEE organised preparatory visits in the pre-study group periods.

Joining a bigger, older society brings up other fears, such as the huge distance between the newcomer and the "leading top", while, in new societies, we meet condensation of generations.

The question of generations appears at the move from study group to provisional society status the latest. The first generation – "who came with the *May-flower*" – invested a lot, created a lot, and worked a lot. They knew what is there to know in psychoanalysis and around the society. The existence of the society is still unsure and under threat, both from inside and from the outside. They have to work almost independently, but the group is young, small, and perceived as weak. Better to stay with what has been proved – persons and organisational functioning. Symptomatic is that handing over the offices and functions seems to be impossible while important; mistrust is in the air toward the next analytic generation – and among the members of the next generation as well. Two types of fear are ubiquitous in the background: (1) the fear that the incoming generation will destroy what had been built up; (2) fear that the founders, the "oldies", will be thrown out and forgotten ungratefully.

Another organisational defence, isolation, serves to ward off the justifiable sense of weakness of a small society. This appears toward the other local psychotherapy, etc., organisations, but also toward the similar neighbouring analytic organisations and the major international associations.

Different studies indicate that choosing analytic training and career is partially motivated by the wish to belong among the "selected ones", and to find a safe place in that community. However, the new, eastern European study groups/societies were born in a period when the survival of psychoanalysis was told to be under threat.

A study group consists of just a handful of people. The site visit evaluates the members and candidates but tries also to assess whether they are willing and capable to develop together into a society which takes care autonomously of the training and maintenance of psychoanalysis. The appointed sponsoring committee invests a lot to mentor such a development. However, a little group is very prone to fall apart, especially when it is overloaded by unlearned tasks and roles, coming from a strange organisational culture – which is IPA – represented by the sponsoring committee. As long as the group is small, the space is also small to meet and handle organisational differences and conflicts; therefore, those appear in the form of personal conflicts. The group must grow to reach an organisational size in which already-smaller groups take shape and carry out intergroup conflicts inside and contained by the forming society. A sign of the problem is that the members take hesitantly roles (such as seminar teaching, executive, training committee, etc., membership). Connected with that, the founding persons remain very long in all leading positions. Symptomatic can be a general dissatisfaction with the officers, the committees, and especially the cooperation between the committees. Growing slows down; the dissatisfaction with the sponsoring committee remains hidden. Another sign could be that the formal and informal structures of the group get frozen.

At the foundation of the new Hungarian study group, the site visit committee recognised five young analysts of that time as direct members – and as training analysts. In the society's slang, until now, they were mentioned not by names but as "The Fives." Of them we elected the presidents, and unquestioned, they functioned as a training committee through 17 years. It was a painful procedure to change the system into a usual rotating one. Today, it is already anecdotical, but the decision – in which order the members will leave the training commit-tee year by year – was done by drawing matches. The deep, unspoken feeling was that it meant also as a "dying order".

Fact is that this period is overstressing and overloading from the organisation's point of view as well, which requires much greater personal investment from the few persons who are at hand. On the personal level, enthusiasm and high com-mitment are the resource; on the organisation's level, membership and trainees' number growing is demanded.

Some Conclusions

The development to growing into a society goes on in the interplay of cohesive and distractive forces. I underline the importance of how much and whether enough containing and holding are available for the individuals and for the group/society during those sensitive years – from inside and from the broader, the international analytic community.

If you meet papers written by analysts on the functioning of analytic socie-ties, the majority is quite ruthlessly critical about their way of being and describes what goes on in individual terminology, sometimes in individual psychopathology. I very much know how extremely difficult it is to look at the problems and crisis also from a group dynamical point of view. Especially difficult is to see distrac-tive events as organisational symptoms and distractive processes as organisational defences.

My – still unanswered – question changed from "What is wrong with psycho-analytic organisations, and how could they be cured?" to "What can be seen as normal developmental conflict, event, or phase? What can be seen as organisational symptom, crisis? What could be good practice and solution?"

During the early phases of development, analytic groups are held together by external and internal forces. The grounding fathers and mothers are enforced exter-nally to work together – to form a society. Early tasks and collisions, if not brought to the surface and handled also as organisational phenomena, remain as uncon-scious "anti-group type of configurations" part of the society; they appear again and again at critical periods – for example, in the form of split repetition. During the early phases, the developing group is small and weak, while the tasks for it are overloading, and the members have to cope with condensation of roles.

It helps if we try to understand the events simultaneously from the personal-interpersonal point of view and as organisational phenomena, fears, and defences, and if we understand what can be seen as a natural, unavoidable part of development.

The most important tool to helping development and to lessen destructive pro-cesses is containing those societies by mentoring and integration into the broader psychoanalytic community. Subregional, regional, and world organisations play an extremely important role; notwithstanding, this possibility is, in my view, underused. And Covid destroyed, to a great extent, those networks. That affords attention for and interest in rearranging those connections.

Notes

1 Working note of the IPA Institutional Issues Task Force (May 2016).
2 PIEE/EPI was founded in 1988 and finished its work in 2023.
3 Both the International Psychoanalytic Association and the European Psychoanalytic Federation set up its helping committees for eastern European countries, which later unified.

References

Gabbard, G., & Ogden, Th. (2009). On becoming an analyst. *International Journal of Psychoanalysis, 90,* 311–327.

Junkers, G., Tuckett, D., & Zachrisson, A. (2008). To be or not to be a psychoanalyst – how do we know a candidate is ready to qualify? Difficulties and controversies in evaluating psychoanalytic competence. *Psychoanalytic Inquiry, 28,* 288–308.

Kutter, P. (Ed.). (1992). *Psychoanalysis international. A guide to psychoanalysis throughout the world* (Vol. 1). Fromman-Holzbog.

Stokoe, Ph. (2011). The healthy and the unhealthy organization: How can we help teams to remain effective? In A. Rubitel & D. Reiss (Eds.), *Containment in the community*. Routledge, Kensaq.

Szőnyi, G., Kardos, T., Stromme, H., & Vassilev, S. (2017). From motivation to organizational integration: Training experiences of recently qualified psychoanalysts. In K. Martin & M. Siegward (Eds.), *Psychology research progress. Psychoanalytic theory: A review and directions for research* (pp. 1–64). Nova Science Publishers.

Part VII

How Do Different Societies Cope With the Disruptions of Their Ideals by Wars and Covid?

Chapter 16

The Shattering of Denials and Disruption of Ideals in the Assumption of Novelties Within Psychoanalytic Organisations

Bernard Chervet

For several years, our group of seven colleagues from different European societies has been meeting in order to share our institutional experiences with other colleagues and to reflect together on the clinical material that emerges within psychoanalytic institutions.

The parameters that determine this clinical material are very difficult to apprehend, since no institution lies down on a couch to associate freely, and they follow the logics of the life of groups. We generally discuss these logics in terms of collective psychology, group mentality, or mass logic. They are modalities of functioning of psychic life that we can also listen to with our patients in our consulting rooms; but other factors play a part in institutions which are linked to their raisons d'être and their missions, thus their ideals: for example, the hope of being able to improve the life of our patients by helping them work on their psychic life, the support and development of psychoanalysis as a therapeutic and scientific discipline, the training of new psychoanalysts, the impact of psychoanalytic spirit in society. Each of these ideals can become the object of an idealisation due to a denial of its limits and of the obstacles that stand in the way of its accomplishment. If psychoanalysis is an impossible profession, sometimes it becomes impossible to practice psychoanalysis, as much for external as internal reasons.

The notion of the historical, social, political, national, regional, and international context has a great deal of importance in this reflection, since all our psychoanalytical organisations have their place within these contexts.

I am proposing that we turn our reflections today towards taking this context and its effects into consideration. Given that it is impossible to bring together all its parameters, and that they have effects that only appear retrospectively, our reflections can only be partial or biased, incomplete and always unfinished, and therefore need to be completed or rectified.

The most obvious recent events that have imposed modifications on the functioning of our organisations are the pandemic of 2020 and the war between Russian and Ukraine that began in 2022.

As far as the pandemic of 2020 is concerned, it served to reveal certain habits and routines that become established within each group and within each of us. The pandemic thus revealed that Western countries were living in denial. In spite of the

DOI: 10.4324/9781032709819-24

warnings of certain scientists, the risks and the danger that a virus could disrupt the Western world were denied. For the West, pandemics belonged to the past, or even to the Middle Ages. Even though the Spanish flu killed 2.5 per cent of the world's population, Western countries have focused their attention and memories on the disruptions and the abominations of the First World War.

This was how pandemics became literary metaphors to refer to other plagues; the key example is Albert Camus's *The Plague*, a book in which the plague metaphorises the dissemination of Nazism. It is worth emphasising that this denial serves to counter another much greater concern, due to the fact that it reminds us of our helplessness, namely, that of the future of our planet and the unlimited use we make of it.

The war between Russia and Ukraine has also been revelatory, not of a similar denial concerning wars, but of an illusion that war in Europe could be permanently avoided thanks to intense reflection and the duty of memory that followed the two world wars of the 20th century, and thanks to the shared concern to prevent the re-establishment of conditions similar to those that permitted the atrocities of the Second World War.

This hope contained an element of illusion. Denial and illusion have been shattered by recent events. The immediate consequence of the pandemic on our profession was the physical distance between analysts themselves and between analysts and their patients, which tangibly awakened our phobias of touching, albeit in different ways for each person. From another point of view, these health measures had an effect of reverberation on our reflections concerning our session work by making us compare the differences between working remotely and working in bodily presence. Our institutions often reacted to this distancing by encouraging their members to share their experiences during remote clinical presentations in which there was a mix of emotional sharing, exchanges concerning the solutions practiced by each analyst, and theoretical reflection on our work, as well as on the traumatic dimension awakened by such an external agent independent of the analytic treatment itself.

Theoretical questions concerned the importance for psychic growth of the presence of the material body. What differences are there between the transference cathexes encouraged and permitted by the presence of the protagonists' bodies and those in their absence? Many remarks were made, varying greatly depending on the clinical situation of each patient; for example, concerning the frequent intensification of forms of autoeroticism during a remote presence, but also concerning the often not very apparent role of perception in the mental functioning during the session of both the analyst and the patient, a role revealed by its lack. All the questions led to developments concerning the differences between the two working methods. The balance between ideation, affects, libidinal excitation, and perceptions had to be reconsidered.

While psychoanalysis, in its early stages, relied on a method whose principle was to diminish the effects and impacts of the stimuli of sensory perception (see Freud's 1904 text "Freud's psycho-analytic procedure", in which he insists on the absence of stimuli from perception), it evolved towards a method that took more account not of the absence of perceptions but rather their stability (which was called the "frame" by J. Bleger). We also need to consider the fact that at the heart of this stability, there is an unapparent use of perception during the sessions. An important difference between the two methods concerns the work of abstinence that must be carried out by analysand and analyst alike, under the aegis of the fundamental rule which requires the analysand to express through language and in his or her free associations everything that crosses their minds; the same holds true for the analyst at the level of his or her reflections and evenly suspended attention. It is a matter, therefore, of questioning ethics, certainly through acts, but also through the session cathexes.

Changes in the conception of trauma as it evolved from the *neurotica* to *Beyond the Pleasure Principle* (Freud, 1920), and then in the work of Freud's successors, were highlighted by our institutions, as were questions relating to the protocol and the method. Take, for example, the major enquiry conducted by the IPA amongst its members concerning "remote analysis", with the question of whether or not the standards of psychoanalytic training should be changed. Consequently, the theorisation of what happens in the session, the theory of technique, is once again changing dramatically.

These high-impact events, stemming from a context that is extraneous to analysis itself, have mobilised our institutions. At what point do such disturbances make analytic work impossible? I am thinking of terrorist attacks and situations of war in certain countries (Lebanon, Israel, Ukraine, etc.).

But they have also taught us that these events resonate with the most silent aspects of our psychic functioning, the tendencies towards neutralisation and extinction that often occur under the cover of manifest productions which have a concealing function in relation to the negative side of these impacts. This may manifest itself by an exacerbation of the intensity of psychic productions or actions as responses to the extinctive and destructive tendencies awakened by the context of disorganisation, but also by reactions of inertia, depression, inhibition, sterilisation, and neutralisation of all intrapsychic tension. Analysis then becomes impossible, but from the inside of psychic lives.

Fortunately, as I have already said, we are also witnessing a call to mentalisation, in several stages, which can open out onto novelties and unusual solutions, onto a creativity that retrospectively sheds a positive light on devastating events.

The example of the pandemic and of the intense reflection on the differences between working in each other's physical presence and working remotely confronts us with two different forms of presence which each has different impacts. The question remains as to whether we can call work that is done uniquely at a distance psychoanalysis, a question that is related to an essential aspect of childhood concerning the resolution of the Oedipus complex: Is the latter realizable in the physical absence of the parents? Oedipal mourning has the specificity of taking place in the presence of the objects that are objects of mourning; the modification pertains to the quality of the cathexes and not to the loss of the external objects. It is a matter of constructing internal objects insofar as they become lost objects, lost for drive activity in favour of mental functioning.

In order to stand back a little from the events referred to, which are all still very topical and have not yet revealed through their deferred effects the meanings of the discourses concerning them, I am going to refer schematically to what happened between 1939 and 1953 in France, at the SPP. The context of those years can be followed in different ways. For example, in 1938, the theme of the Congress for French-Speaking Psychoanalysts was "masochism"; between 1939 and 1947, the congresses did not take place. During this time, the SPP closed its doors and suspended all its activities. It reopened after the war, and in 1948, the theme of the first French-language congress was "aggressiveness". It is difficult not to notice the determining relation between the general context, worldwide here, and the themes of the congresses. The same is true for the EPF conference: "realities", "ideals", "illusions". And before the current war, the IPA had chosen for next year "mind in the line of fire".

In 1945, the resumption of all activities in France and in Europe, and even in the world, created a period which in Europe we call the "baby boom". This effect did not spare psychoanalysis and its societies. The SPP found itself faced with a surge of requests for treatment and potential candidates for analytic training. A reflection conducted in conjunction with the IPA led to modifications of the Eitingon model used by the SPP since 1926. These modifications were motivated, therefore, by pragmatic, contextual, and temporary reasons. This was how analytic training sessions were reduced from 1 hour to 3/4 hour, and the number of weekly sessions for a training analysis from five or four to three sessions; furthermore, these criteria were also applied to analyses supervised during training, and the solution of group supervision was invented. All these criteria had the aim of producing a larger number of analysts for the same amount of work/time.

A crisis then occurred within the SPP and led to the 1953 split over the question of the reorganisation of the training institute. It was a question of deciding if the institute should provide a university-style training, if it should be run by doctors, or if the training should be linked to other broader criteria. Retrospectively, we can say it was a matter of managing a difference, that of the generations, a central question within our institutions.

The training modifications promoted by the context were thus in no way the reasons for the split. Nor are they at the origin of the *French model*, contrary to what we are accustomed to thinking. The French model arose gradually, and much later, from a reflection that was induced, it is true, by these contextual changes, but which concerned the strict separation of functions, the separation between the personal analysis (with the suppression of the notion of training analysis in 1972) and the training programme. The fundamental element which explains the creation of the French model was the critique of the analyst's involvement in the training process. The principle on which the creation of the French model was based is the differentiation and separation of functions. The critique pertained, above all, to "reporting", but also to the fact that it could seem strange to select a future analyst who had not yet conducted a psychoanalytic treatment, thus not to relate the request for analysis to personal suffering, to private symptomatology, and to the wish to modify one's psychic functioning. The French model considers that we have all been, even before becoming psychoanalysts, patients who had personal reasons to seek help and treatment in psychoanalysis. The transference onto psychoanalysis turns out to contain this therapeutic expectation.

It thus seems possible to think of the crisis of 1953 as an after-effect of the traumatic extinctive tendencies awakened by the war itself, masked by the euphoria of the baby boom, but also of the death of Freud, whose mourning was put into abeyance due to the circumstances.

It was thus on the basis of the difference of generations, and induced by the pragmatic and concrete aspects of training, that this reflection on training called into question the Eitingon model until the French model was recognised by the IPA in 2005, thus 60 years after the contextual changes of the protocol. A first context of disappearance paved the way for another context of rebirth, of a change of generation, thus of mourning and generativity, with modifications of the training criteria. Out of these two stages, a reflection arose on training which reconnected with the state of mind of the fundamental rule of psychoanalysis, in particular, with the part that concerns the analyst: complete candour for the patient, strict discretion for the analyst.

References

Freud, S. (1904). *Freud's psycho-analytic procedure. SE* (Vol. 7, pp. 249–254).
Freud, S. (1920). *Beyond the pleasure principal. SE* (Vol. 18, pp. 1–64).

Chapter 17

Ideals, Unconscious Beliefs, and Leadership in Times of Covid and Conflict

Philip Stokoe

Our forum has enabled us to meet with a significant number of societies in Europe, all of whom have their own personality and their own history, but it has also been possible to recognise common themes. These themes have led to similar tensions within a wide range of societies, some of them leading to splits, others requiring effort to retain different views within the same society. As I described earlier in this book, I think this reflects two problems endemic to psychoanalytic institutions, both of which are consequences of the way in which Freud encouraged the development of separate societies which led to the international psychoanalytic association.

The move from his waiting room to a venue representing a more institutional identity was resisted powerfully. The way that I have described this is the move from an entrepreneurial system to a managed system. Those of us who work with organisations will encounter this challenge on a regular basis. There is always resistance; therefore, the change requires some resilience, but commercial organisations mostly manage the move successfully; very few psychoanalytic institutions have done so. As I remarked earlier, a ubiquitous feature of dysfunction in an organisation or group is that it always feels *personal*.

One could argue that there is a compelling similarity to the move from the pleasure principle to the reality principle, a move that I consider to be the same as the Kleinian idea of the move from paranoid-schizoid to depressive position (Klein, 1946). My own view, following Bion (1962) and Fisher (2006), is that this is only possible because human beings have developed a curiosity drive at the same level as those of love and hate. In other words, it is one of the innate or primary drives that build the conscious, cognitive, self-reflective mind. I mention this now because it follows that, if the stimulation of curiosity propels the individual towards facing reality, then the retreat to the pleasure principle or paranoid schizoid position closes down curiosity so that certainty will prevail (Stokoe, 2020).

I make this comparison to a developmental stage because I think that the reason for such a strong resistance to the move into a managed system is the pleasure that each member of an organisation gets from having direct access to the leader, like direct access to the mother. We all know that this shape is unsustainable after the organisation reaches a certain size. Instead, it is necessary to set up some form

DOI: 10.4324/9781032709819-25

of hierarchical system in which tasks can be carried out by specialist parts of the organisation in the service of a centrally created strategy. Given the unconscious fear of losing a structure in which everyone is directly connected to the "leader", one of the ways that organisations can avoid the move into a properly managed system is to transform what might be described in other contexts as directorates or departments into mini entrepreneurial systems. Thus, the training function in one of our institutions can shape itself around the chair of something usually described as a committee. Separately – and admissions committee will function in a similar way – all members gather around a single leader. When these systems work well, it is almost entirely down to personal relationships between chairs of committees.

I do not intend to go any further into the theory or analysis of the shapes of our institutions, but I need to define my use of one more concept before I discuss external threats.

Ideal

For me, this term refers to a state of perfection; indeed the *Collins English Dictionary* defines it as "a conception of something that is perfect, especially that which one seeks to attain." Of course, in this way, Freud's concept of ego ideal provides a model to which to aspire. However, the point that I want to make is that perfection is impossible; the concept belongs to the paranoid schizoid position, in which the split is between ideal good and ideal bad, not simply good and bad. In this state of mind for the baby, mother is perfect, and identification with her fills the baby with a sense of omnipotence. In the Kleinian idea of development, to which I subscribe, the key moment, crucial to the development of the reality position, is the ability to acknowledge the loss of this ideal and to mourn that loss. To put it another way, the reality position requires the capacity to be aware that the ideal is a distortion of something normal and that normal is part of the world that is continually changing and developing.

I want to propose that there is another kind of ideal, one that operates much more powerfully than a shared and recognised one. Not surprisingly, as a psychoanalyst, I am referring to something unconscious. This time unconscious beliefs. Once again, I need to crave your indulgence so that I can refer to something that I have spoken about in other places, that is, an unconscious belief that was passed on from Freud to all of us and which is often incorporated with tremendous power into our institutions. We all know that Freud had an ambition that psychoanalysis should be accepted by universities and that universities should teach psychoanalysis and train psychoanalysts. However, at the same time that he was seeking to develop the wider psychoanalytic community, he was forced to conclude that universities would not teach psychoanalysis and train psychoanalysts because of anti-Semitism. He therefore asked the job of teaching and training future psychoanalysts to psychoanalytic institutions. Although he did this regretfully, I think it has been taken as the last wish of the dying father so that it has become an organising belief at an unconscious level in our institutions. You can see evidence of this in the language used about trainings which often includes expressions like the gold standard. In other words, an ideal. However, if it were an ideal that could be recognised to be impossible, it would be so much easier to change the nature of our trainings in the light of changes in our societies and cultures. The fact that any suggested change arouses passions suggests that this comes from an unconscious identification rather than something that can be thought about.

All this brings us to the question of how our institutions have responded to external threats.

Command and Control

The functioning of an executive committee with a strong leader can be very effective in times of trouble. For example, the often-misunderstood concept of command and control that derives from military activity can be extremely effective in times of crisis. Of course, it can also be extremely dangerous if the leadership is unable to value information coming from outside. History provides us with many examples of these two different kinds of leadership; one is the comparison between Dwight D. Eisenhower and General Douglas MacArthur. Both were very successful generals in the Second World War, but much to the chagrin in MacArthur, it was Eisenhower who was made Supreme Allied Commander and who masterminded the D-Day landings. The UK equivalent of MacArthur was Montgomery, about whom Churchill famously said, "In defeat, unbeatable; in victory unbearable." MacArthur and Montgomery were incredibly good strategists in the delivery of military success, but it was a narcissistic achievement. You could say that the two *M*s shared a style of leadership that was summed up by Montgomery, who had nothing good to say about Eisenhower, claiming, "[H]e had no plan of his own . . . Eisenhower held conferences to collect ideas; I held conferences to issue orders".

The truth is that Eisenhower worked on the principle that the best decisions require the best information, and he encouraged a system of letting information pass up the hierarchy. This way, he was able to create the D-Day landing plans. Equally, in the other direction, he was not threatened by passing decision-making authority down the line. His message was, "This is the overall aim, but to achieve it, I shall rely on you to make decisions on the ground that are a response to what you find there".

I can really only speak about my society when it comes to Covid. In fact, it was very impressive how the society managed this situation. Able very quickly to recognise the importance of moving online, the board managed to set up advisory meetings available for all members to talk about current understanding of the Covid threat. This involved meetings with senior people within the NHS and the public health services. There were also extra meetings to offer views about how to manage during lockdown.

The biggest challenge was to support colleagues in finding a way to provide psychoanalysis without the physical presence of patients. The society had already set up the online provision of lectures and courses for the general public, so there was already some expertise, and this expertise was made available to members of the society. Meanwhile, the online provision of lectures, seminars, webinars, and discussions became extremely popular. I think this was a global phenomenon, and several of us found ourselves delivering lectures that would previously have been addressing a maximum of 60 people to a virtual crowd of over 300.

I think this was an example of the Eisenhower form of leadership. Nobody knew about Covid, so it was perfectly sensible and reasonable to seek advice from outside and from the membership. This kind of leadership meant that ideas were made available very quickly and could be disseminated very quickly. It interests me that the development of the vaccine required changing the normal scientific approach of testing because it was felt to be unethical in the face of so many deaths, as well as taking too much time. In the same way, institutions across the world moved very quickly to conducting analyses and trainings of candidates remotely/online. You could say that similar pressures applied; it was necessary to be able to provide psychoanalytic treatments, particularly at a time of international crisis, even though there had been no time to measure the effect difference of such a form of treatment.

Of course, this creates an interesting problem for societies like my own who had rushed straight to the provision online and yet who had reacted with such speed and certainty to the IPA change to the Eitingon principles of frequency of psychoanalysis. The rush to defend four- and five-times-a-week psychoanalysis gave no room for any other views, particularly from those of us who felt that there was a social context that might be thought of as the unconscious stimulus for this sort of change.

In terms of the current situation, there is a wide range of responses to the provision of psychoanalysis online. Most people can see how important it is to be physically present; indeed, the absence of physical contact in the wider world of work has created a huge increase in the provision of antidepressants.

For the moment, I want to look at the way that the entrepreneurial shape enables dangerous blockages to thinking in the form of the impact of unconscious beliefs. This arises in at least two places; I am thinking of the responses to conflicts, not only Russia and Ukraine. I am also thinking of the way that the collapse of thinking in the larger world in the face of gender identity politics has resulted in complete silence – well, not complete; there are a few people out there standing up for the place of scientific thinking. But surprisingly few, given the enormity of its implications.

The problem with addressing conflict is that the intensity immediately arouses anxiety. The anxiety tends to pull us into a paranoid-schizoid state of mind, in which certainty masquerades as the solution. My institution, like many others, has responded rapidly to provide support and funding for those in Ukraine. It is very difficult to avoid the invitation to think in black-and-white terms, particularly when Putin's invasion is so shocking and so vicious. On the other hand, we know from colleagues who have been providing support to mediation and conflict, for example, in Israel and Palestine, and in the troubles in Northern Ireland, that the intervention with the greatest hope for a resolution is one that asks each protagonist to try to understand the mind and beliefs of the other side. Of course, we do this all the time with our patients, with the aim of introducing a new way of understanding an internal conflict that has remained stuck because of unconscious beliefs. The state of mind that I am describing is one that seeks an external authority that makes everything better, a dependent state of mind. Bion describes this as one of his basic assumption modes, in other words, a defensive internal organisation within a group that aims to reduce anxiety.

The only way to free ourselves from this trap is to maintain the capacity to think about the meaning of the beliefs on each side of the conflict.

During this same period of Covid and of conflict, I was involved with a series of lectures that had been running successfully before lockdown. The aim of the lectures was to bring a psychoanalytic mind to political and social problems. This series went online during lockdown and suddenly attracted an international audience in the hundreds. One would be forgiven for thinking that this sort of webinar, in which the audience was encouraged to participate, might be very welcome at such a time. However, the very executive committee which had acted so well to adapt and support the membership to adapting to the pandemic and then to the invasion of Ukraine became very anxious about these lectures. It was clear that the focus on the analysis of conflict and of the move to the right of governments imposing lockdown was the cause of this anxiety. To be more accurate, audience members had reacted to the discussion of how beliefs guide governments dealing with the pandemic or those in conflict as if such a *discussion* were itself racist or blaming. The reaction of the executive was to move into that misunderstanding of "command and control" exhibited by Montgomery and MacArthur; it sought to rescind the delegation of decision-making about the content of these public lectures and control that directly from the centre.

Fortunately, a robust discussion about this led to a restatement of the delegation of the authority to make such decisions to the lecture series committee.

The reason for describing this event is to observe some of the processes that I claim to be quite easily activated when there is an organisational rise in anxiety interpreted as a fear of attack, leading to a retreat to a paranoid-schizoid state in which there is an attempt to defend an ideal. In this case, the executive had moved very quickly to support online psychoanalysis. But this was the same executive which had moved with little debate to challenge the IPA change to the Eitingon principles, so an organisational consultant might hypothesise that there was already a tendency towards maintaining an entrepreneurial shape by encouraging a dependent unconscious defensive mode. The lecture series then appeared as the means through which an attack could be made against unconsciously held ideals. So it was necessary to establish control over this danger. The external world of conflict aroused an unconscious fear of internal conflict.

In the same way, those who feel that psychoanalytic colleagues in Russia should take a more active role in exposing Putin's lies about the war against Ukraine speak from a perfectly understandable position; however, it makes it extremely difficult even to begin to engage in understanding how it feels to be a Russian psychoanalyst at this time. I think that the arousal of the dependent state of mind in our institutions makes it very difficult for the entrepreneurial system to free itself. Douglas MacArthur waged his war in the role of the father who knew what was right and required everybody else to follow his example. The default shape of our psychoanalytic institutions makes us vulnerable to this same sort of dynamic.

It is worth noting that the forum that facilitates this chapter is in the same position vis-à-vis the EPF, and that lecture series was in relation to the institute. It is not without irony that we might observe that the organisational equivalent of the psychoanalytic position in the consulting room, that of maintaining a space for enquiry, can quickly become identified with an attack on the ideal that forms part of the unconscious identity of the psychoanalytic organisation. The maintenance of an attitude of benign enquiry requires constant vigilance because it can collapse so quickly.

References

Bion, W. R. (1962). A theory of thinking. *International Journal of Psychoanalysis*, *43*, 306–310.

Fisher, J. V. (2006). The emotional experience of K. *International Journal of Psychoanalysis*, *87*, 1221–1237.

Klein, M. (1952). Notes on some schizoid mechanisms. *The International Journal of Psychoanalysis*, *27*, 99–110. [Updated in: Klein, M. *Envy and gratitude and other works (1946–1963). Writings of Melanie Klein* (Vol. III, pp. 1–24). Hogarth Press (Development)]. (Original work published 1946)

Stokoe, P. (2020). *The curiosity drive: Our need for inquisitive thinking*. Phoenix Publishing House.

Part VIII

Psychoanalytic Organisations Caught in the Crossfire

Chapter 18

Psychoanalytic Organisations Caught in the Crossfire

Group Psychologies Revealed

Bernard Chervet

Psychoanalytic organisations are caught in the crossfire. They are influenced by the external context, that is, by the political, social, cultural, and health context, which is infinite by nature, but they are also places where more mysterious psychic mindsets are revealed that are only expressed in groups. These mindsets emerge as soon as people are in a group and delegate to the group the task of providing them with solutions to reduce their traumatic experiences. To do this, they draw on the external context but are also at the origin of the external configurations – found/created – that they need to fulfil their anti-traumatic function. These configurations are often attributed to the external context and not recognised as realities promoted by group mindsets.

Each organisation is marked by the contextual circumstances of its origin; by what motivated its foundation, its participation in the development of psychoanalysis, and its presence in new territories; by the personalities of its founders and the charisma bestowed on them by the group; and by the cultural, therapeutic, and political ideals concealed within the official investment in psychoanalysis. But it reveals psychological functions that can only exist in a group, functions that we call collective psychology, group mentality, mass psychology, etc.

It is not possible, of course, to reduce individual psychology to internal reasons and collective psychology to external causes. While sociology brings its own intelligibility to social phenomena, psychoanalysis is in a position to propose a specific approach because collective, group, and mass psychologies are an integral part of individual psychology, as potentialities, through the identifications involved in the foundations of psychic life.

Group psychologies correspond to specific psychic functions that exist potentially in each individual but which only come to light within a group and when a group solution is found by all the members of the group to respond to the traumatic quality experienced by each of them. The change in psychic functioning should then be seen as a distortion rather than a regression, a distortion that is in conflict with the ability to be alone in the presence of others (Winnicott), that is, to preserve individual psychic functioning.

The idea of creating the IPA came about in 1908 in a context of dissension, defection, and deviations that had emerged among the pioneers of the Psychological

DOI: 10.4324/9781032709819-27

Wednesday Society founded in 1902, dissension in particular with Adler and his *individual psychology* based on *compensation* and *virile protest*. The IPA was founded in 1910; Adler resigned in 1911, and Stekel in 1912.

The primary motivation for creating the IPA was Freud's concern, shared by Jones, to support psychoanalysis as a science against deviations from the metapsychological corpus that had arisen within the first group of analysts. To this end, it was decided to bring psychoanalysts together regularly at an international congress.

History tells us that this safeguard, the creation of an international body and a community of members, was not enough (Freud, 1913). As early as 1912, new dissensions arose between Freud and Jung. In 1914, having recently been re-elected as president of the IPA, Jung resigned from his post. A few months later, the Zurich Psychoanalytical Society withdrew from the IPA. Since then, this society has remained independent of the Swiss Psychoanalytical Society, and therefore of the IPA. Faced with persistent threats to the psychoanalytical corpus and to the practice of psychoanalysis, Jones once again proposed (though in opposition to the exoterism at the origin of the IPA) the creation of a secret committee made up of a few members of the IPA. This esoteric committee served as a rearguard that was supposed to guarantee the fundamental principles of psychoanalytic theory. Its function required it to be independent of the IPA establishment. Once again, this was a temporary solution. In 1923, it was Rank who introduced a new distortion with the *birth trauma* and its technical consequences. He was replaced by Anna Freud. Nepotism reared its head, and the separation of powers that had been desired at the outset, between the establishment (the administrative side) and the Secret Committee (the scientific side), was no longer respected once Jones had become president in 1920. In 1927, the Committee was dissolved.

After the First World War, what predominated was the dissemination of psychoanalysis through translation and publishing. Then, from 1926 onwards, the organisation and standardisation of training, together with the question of lay analysis, became the IPA's main concerns. These questions then crystallised into a conflict between Europe and North America. We still have some traces of this with the exceptionalism of the APsaA.

It would be interesting to follow the evolution of the parameters that presided over the birth of the IPA, as well as their inclusion within the missions that the IPA has considered to be its own from its origins to the present day. Today, the IPA considers that it has a role to play in the mental health of human beings throughout the world, and that it must become involved in social issues, which was not the case when it was founded. This involvement is supposed to be with reference to psychoanalysis. But this qualifier is caught in the crossfire of politicisation, corporatism, and charitable benevolence.

History, therefore, contains determinants that we, at the IMF (Institutional Matter Forum), are trying to identify and which play a part in multifactorial overdetermination.

Taking history into account allows us to follow the evolution of the orientations of our organisations and to look for the internal reasons, while taking into account a fact that differentiates our groups from all the others, namely, that the members of our organisations have had personal experience of analysis. The question arises as to whether the modes of functioning revealed in groups are accessible through session work.

The way our institutions operate is a reflection of what scientists now call "complex systems", where irreducible singularity dominates. While the science of complex systems emphasises above all the unpredictability of emergence, psychoanalysis also attaches great importance to repetition, the compulsions of repetition and reduction, and the two-stage organisation of human thought according to the operation of après-coup. *Overdetermination* is defined by recognising the influence of the goals to be achieved (Aristotle's final cause), goals which combine unconscious ideals with the official goal of all our organisations, the development of psychoanalysis.

It is certainly possible to identify some of the effects of the great traumas of history on our organisations, their interruptions, their more or less temporary disappearances, their rebirths in various forms, etc. It is less easy to grasp the resurgence after the event, through conflicts, crises, splits, and ethical issues, or to understand how the revitalisation and innovations that follow take place. It is not so easy to grasp the resurgences of these events retrospectively through conflicts, crises, and splits, or to understand how the revitalisation and innovations that follow are brought about.

The disturbances caused by Covid, for example, revealed a lack of reflection on the influence of the presence of the body on the way the two protagonists functioned during the session, on the work of abstinence, and on the involvement of perception in response to the regression to traumatic elements induced during the session. Remote analysis has become an object of reflection, as has the notion of ideal psychic functioning.

Another example concerns the emergence of the French model as an après-coup of the trauma of the Second World War. The re-establishment of the separation of functions, but this time between analysis and training, used the springboard of the modifications to the classic protocol of the analytic treatment that occurred just after the war in agreement with the IPA for pragmatic reasons linked to the baby boom. It took about 15 years for the double principle of personal analysis, as opposed to training analysis, and of the separation of personal analysis and training, as opposed to reporting, to emerge as the French model, and another 50 years for this model to be enshrined in the rules of the IPA.

In the two aforementioned cases, the two factors, traumatic factors (health, war) and generativity, are recognisable.

Any conception of the traumatic factor is attracted by the most commonplace reaction, which consists in placing the reason for the trauma outside the subject. Like the *neurotica*, the infantile mindsets of phobias take over. They respond to internal unconscious dynamics and related anxieties by transposing them onto external, perceivable, and tangible objects. This externalisation helps maintain repression, transform anxiety into an objectifiable danger, and initiate protective measures against the outside world; but these transpositions also allow the repressed to return in the form of substitutes, hence the possibility of reintegration and an elaboration that enriches individual functioning.

The belief that this is an external danger enables children to defend themselves against their terrors, nightmares, and anxiety. Parents respond by maintaining the latent correlation between the object that serves as a support for the transposition and the unconscious internal world, thereby offering opposition to the internal threat.

It is this dynamic that we most frequently observe in our sessions, when unconscious material is expressed through free association, in the form of discourse about scenes from our patients' present or even past lives. Psychoanalytic interpretation works in reverse. It goes in search of regressive unconscious material with a strong power to attract disorganisation and hopes to obtain the dissolution of anxiety through awareness involving language. The therapeutic effect is based on this elaboration.

Two approaches emerge implicitly that we use in our day-to-day work. One advocates elaboration, that is, psychic work aimed at bringing unconscious contents and tendencies into consciousness; the other seeks to reinforce opposition to anxiety and the extinctive attraction characteristic of the drives.

What is valid for an individual is only an analogy for a group. A group does not come and lie on a couch. To confuse the functioning of an individual psyche with that of a group does not seem very fruitful to us, unless we attribute to the group a psychic life as such.

The singular personal dynamics of a psyche, organised by an oscillatory interplay between daytime and night-time activities, between sleeping-dreaming and social life, between work and eroticism, has no equivalent in group dynamics. Regression to the psychic activities that regenerate passivity, dreaming, and free association only exists in the individual. The notion of regression is not applicable to the change in mental functioning that occurs when an appeal is made to collective mindsets. The term *regression* suggests a continuity between the cruelty of the "collective mind" and the sadism of the individual, as well as between the masochism of the individual and the mass submission of the collective mind, even though they refer to different ideals and idealisations of these ideals.

In groups, individual regression gives way to other ways of functioning, to distortions that we call collective, group, or mass psychology. Recourse to group solutions favours the path of dissolution rather than that of elaboration.

In our group, we have often been astonished by the gap that exists between the most pertinent reflections on how groups function and the specific courses of action that can be taken within them, with differences depending on whether the group is a couple, a family, a small or large group, and whether it is driven by more or less implicit situational preoccupations and ideologies.

The intelligibility of group actions provided by the concepts of collective psychology, group psychology, group mentality, mass psychology, and communities based on hysterical identification, narcissistic mutuality, or reinforcement of denial does not resolve the gap between the relevance of discourse and the group phenomena themselves. Language does not seem to be enough to modify group actions any more than the possibility of identifying individually with group mindsets outside of group circumstances; let us not forget the gap that exists between a serial killer and genocide!

Our astonishment is as much about the potentialisation of intensity as it is about the conformism that is liable to develop within groups.

Collective, group, and mass psychologies correspond to potential constellations belonging to individual psychology that can only be revealed and expressed in specific circumstances: within a group and when individual traumatic neuroses turn to the group to find solutions together to remove the extinctive tendency of the drives involved in traumatic neurosis. Freud wrote *Group Psychology and the Analysis of the Ego* (Freud, 1921) just after *Beyond the Pleasure Principle* (Freud, 1920), just after he had realised that the elementary quality of all drives is their tendency to return to an earlier state of things, even to the inorganic state, a tendency that expresses itself in traumatic neurosis and the compulsions of repetition and reduction. The potential functions of collective, group, and mass psychologies are then brought into play. What is avoided here is the individual masochism aroused by the various renunciations involved in psychic life.

In order to avoid unpleasure, the members of a group can resort to hysterical identification and together support hallucinatory wish fulfilment. The ideal of this collective psychology is to escape the pain of Oedipal mourning in a concealed way.

In the case of group mentality, the aim is to pool narcissisms in order to avoid experiences of incompleteness and vexation and to rediscover infantile experiences of omnipotence. Each member is a narcissistic complement to the other members, hence narcissistic object relations and commensalities. A corporation is formed based on a common ideal of completeness, taking each member back to His Majesty the Baby.

In mass psychology, all the members point to the same external object as being responsible for the traumatic quality, with the common aim of making it disappear through the group potentiation of destructiveness. The denial of perceivable lacks is guaranteed by this theory and the consequent eradication. However, what is abolished on the inside comes back from the outside. This is how destruction nourishes traumatic perceptions while demonstrating that these experiences are, indeed, of external origin. The group then organises itself into a community of denial based on an ideal, a world free of lack.

All these constellations are based on two modes of identification: vertical identification with an ideal, and horizontal identification with the members of the group based on this identification with the same ideal.

The question now arises as to whether confrontation with group mindsets, through our interest in institutional life, and more particularly in the life of psychoanalytic institutions, enables us to better understand, within analysis sessions, potential group psychologies and the ideals to which they refer.

While psychoanalysts cannot become and rebecome psychoanalysts on their own, they do find, through their association with groups, both a support for maintaining their psychoanalytic ideal and the possibility of abandoning their individual analytical functioning in favour of the collective functioning considered ideal by the group.

This brings us back to the opening words of this contribution, concerning the fact that external reality undoubtedly has major effects on our psyches, but that the notion of context includes the use that the mind makes of it and, above all, the fact that the mind seeks-finds-creates the external realities that it needs, especially when it needs to resort to solutions that are only revealed within groups, in correlation with the traumatic quality.

We are used to the idea that our social institutions are created in the image of the "great institutions of the ego" of the individual psyche, that the institutions of justice, the police, medicine, social welfare, child protection, art and culture reflect the fallibility of our psychic functioning. The result is an interplay of internal and external worlds.

Since the middle of the 20th century, the most important concerns of human beings, those relating to what puts us in the greatest danger, are supposed to be created by man. Hence the need to reflect on what it is in us, and which is revealed in groups, that intensifies the danger and brings it back from the outside. The proposals set out earlier suggest that, in this way, we are trying individually to avoid facing up to the endogenous traumatic quality.

This dynamic emerged very clearly in the 20th century, following the repeated abominations of various wars and genocides. It is currently being debated in the form of a conception supported by many scientists, but rejected by others, concerning the mutation of the human race and the planet. This conception highlights the risk of the extinction of our species created by group psychologies. Freud hypothesised as much in 1932 in "Why War?": "It [the cultural process] may perhaps be leading to the extinction of the human race, for in more than one way it impairs the sexual function" (Freud, 1933/1932, p. 214). The regressive tendency to extinguish all instinctual drives is, in fact, involved in our basic traumatic neuroses and in the fact that we turn to the solutions of group psychologies, that is, the abolition of traumatic experiences by acts of mass destruction concerning all human beings, or even the human species.

Numerous teams of researchers around the world envisage the end of the Holocene, a geological period that began around 11,000 years ago. According to them, the Holocene could be dying out, making way for the Anthropocene, characterised by a massive extinction of animal and plant species, an extinction created for the first time by human culture.

The end of the Holocene is thought to have begun in the middle of the 20th century, following the effects of nuclear testing and the misuse of the planet's resources. A century ago, in 1920, Colin N. Waters, the geologist responsible for research into the Anthropocene, wrote "Nature's too big for humans to influence".

The scientists who are currently warning of the end of the Holocene are putting together numerous arguments to support their thesis, without being certain of the validity of their hypothesis or of the creative transformation of an Anthropocene.

A dividing line is drawn between those who consider that mass extinction is occurring without the creation of a new period being assured and those who consider that a new age of man is emerging.

Psychoanalysis envisages that intrapsychic mutations are based on a founding murder, which modifies the past and gives rise to a future. This rationale is found in the resolution of the Oedipus complex, but also in the organisation of groups and the creation of group mentalities.

These final thoughts take us back to the role of the unconscious ideals shared in groups, ideals that are at the root of members' recourse to group psychologies and their consequences. Overdetermination includes the plurality of causalities, plural determinations, but also the fact that a goal to be achieved, an unconscious ideal, can have a major effect on the development of a group, on its orientations and vicissitudes. The power of these unconscious ideals goes far beyond the ideal we all share and which officially defines all our institutions, the preservation and development of psychoanalysis as a science and therapeutic method.

References

Freud, S. (1913). *On psycho-analysis. SE* (Vol. 12, pp. 207–211).
Freud, S. (1920). *Beyond the pleasure principle. SE* (Vol. 18, pp. 1–64).
Freud, S. (1921). *Group psychology and the analysis of the ego. SE* (Vol. 18, pp. 65–143).
Freud, S. (1933). *Why war? SE* (Vol. 22, pp. 195–215). (Original work published 1932)

Chapter 19

Psychoanalytic Organisations in a Time of Crisis

A Survey Report[1]

Jasminka Šuljagić

The survey "Psychoanalytic Organisations in a Time of Crisis" was organised by the EPF Institutional Matters Forum (IMF) and sent to all the societies of the European Psychoanalytic Federation (EPF) in the period from March 2022 till the beginning of 2023. The survey consists of five questions about the major internal crisis/crises that the societies have gone through in their histories, as well as the impact of major global crises: World War II, the Covid-19 crisis, the war in Ukraine, and an open question about other crises and their impact. Each raised item includes an enquiry into the influence of those crises, the means used to deal with and overcome them, and the ongoing consequences for the life of the societies. Confidentiality was guaranteed, and the report with conclusions was announced, but without mentioning any particular society.

Survey

Of the 42 EPF societies, including component societies, provisional societies, and study groups, we received responses from 27 societies, which is almost two-thirds of the total number. It was not an easy process, since, on a number of occasions, the survey had to be sent repeatedly, both from the EPF administrative secretary and from members of our group. The reactions of the presidents were very different, from recognition of the importance of such a project to mistrust or negligence.

The manner in which the responses to the questions were written also varied grossly. From detailed descriptions to very short notes, from elaborated thinking, including the time dimension and various threads, to very restricted answers. Some replies were vague and evasive – "There were at some levels a few conflicts", "Following the crisis which had something to do with this fact" – while some were sincere and called for additional confidence. Elaborative and thoughtful, short and informative, all the responses were very useful.

Internal Crises

On the question whether, in the history of the society, it has ever gone through a major internal crisis/crises, several responses were negative, and at the other end of the spectrum, there are societies which originated in crisis (splits, separations,

DOI: 10.4324/9781032709819-28

conflicts) and those recognising that crisis is inevitable and inherent in the very foundations.

The main sources of the internal crises follow.

Foundational Matters

Certain societies were founded by members leaving previous societies; in some of them, the entire first generation of psychoanalysts was in analysis with one and the same analyst.

Some founding members went through a crisis with long periods of disagreements and conflicts, and/or they remained distanced since they belonged to different backgrounds.

In some of the societies, the founding member left a complex and difficult legacy to the society, and sometimes the death of the founder(s) initiated a crisis, or it was a "silent crisis" in extreme idealisation of the founding masters, never fully elaborated and overcome.

There were also instances of deadlock over the transition of official roles from the founders to new generations (*generational change*).

Ethical Issues

Ethical problems which had remained hidden and unresolved were reported. When disclosed, they were often denied or declared to be a political problem or the result of technical mistakes/breaches. Conflict with the ethics committee developed and took on an institutional nature. Racial discrimination also belongs to this category.

Power Issues, Authoritarian Structure ↔ Absence of Structure and Boundaries

The manifestations of this source of crises go through extremes, from authoritarian structure, abuse of authority, problems with the hierarchic organisation of a society and power conflicts among members, to crises which were lasting and amplified by the absence of a clear society structure.

Models of Training, Training Standards

There are variations from "collapse of training standards, with denial and lies", which inflamed the crisis of the society, towards those aroused by what are considered demanding, outdated, and unnecessary standards. Change in the number of training analysts, either suddenly growing or decreasing, was reported as balance-disruptive. This happens occasionally in connection with another item of importance: *the aging of a society.*

Relations With Other Societies and Other Institutions

The role of psychoanalytic psychotherapy questions what is "properly psychoanalytic".

Decrease in the Number of Members

Several societies reported decreases in numbers as the potential source of crisis.

Independently from the survey questions, a matter of history arose: Do we know the histories of our societies, and does history matter? This knowledge includes not only previous crises but also the development of the societies, and those members who contributed to this. Connected with this is also the question whether we can speak about our history.

Conclusions regarding the consequences of and possible solutions to the main internal crises are:

- Usually, the same patterns repeat themselves through the history of the society.
- An increasing effect of unresolved crises appears: "a lack of appetite for involvement in group activities and a difficulty to rally around clinical/theoretical work", "general apathy towards various scientific and organisational activities", followed by the "impossibility of appointing and electing a new executive board for many months", and similar: "there was no candidate willing to run for the post of president".
- Frequent "attempts to solve problems" are complaints, which have the characteristic of multiplying once they have been raised, then followed by resignations and splits in the societies.
- Certain societies reported that they have resolved previous crises, some of them with the help of a third party: IPA committees, outside consultants, or colleagues from abroad; helpful influence could also be expected from "new generations", an "influx of fresh blood", and "candidates". Some societies lean on internal resources: "a frank exchange of views", discussions, studies, and institutional debates; "the establishment of a continuous climate of institutional debate"; "concentrated effort to deal with controversial discussions"; recognition of repeating patterns, slowly evolving and developing organisational knowledge and administrative procedures, further elaboration of a procedural ethics code, wider comprehension of rules, introducing seminars on ethics.
- There is a recognition that group tensions in the society are both healthy and disruptive, and that only afterwards can we learn what was becoming from the current crises, without a final conclusion, only forming new suppositions about their origin and influences, which is a path of institutional thinking and transformation.

Second World War

Many of the EPF societies were founded after WWII, but barely any remain unaffected by it to some extent, if in different ways.

For the societies under the direct impact of the war, those years were "a catastrophic break in history"; societies were dissolved or did not manage to preserve their organisational independence, and many analysts were murdered or expelled by the National Socialist regime. S. Freud and his family were forced into exile in London. After 1945, there was a slow revival of psychoanalysis, with a concerted effort to deal with the traumatic consequences of the war, with the formation, reconstruction, or re-establishment of the societies, mourning and reflection on Freud's legacy.

In several societies, the initial development of psychoanalytic ideas was obstructed, either by occupation at the beginning of the war or by regime change immediately after the war period. The other dictatorship regimes of that time, and their consequences, are similarly described.

Certain data or reports which appeared after the war about society members brought about new tensions and challenges for organisational cohesion and became retroactively an issue of discussion.

Even societies formed after WWII and beyond the war area reported the "impact of a previous generation, in terms of resistance or loyalty".

Covid-19 Crisis

Almost all respondent societies struggled to continue functioning, thinking about changed conditions regarding psychoanalytical, organisational, and training issues. This is the big difference compared to the WWII situation, where individual analysts' solidarity was at stake: now the organisation showed its potential. This will be especially true when we come to the next question about war in Ukraine, but it is also prominent in the Covid-19 context.

Many exchanges, seminars, presentations, and discussions were organised by a majority of the societies concerning the impact of the pandemic situation.

In general, most of the societies responded that the pandemic does not seem to have initiated any serious destabilising group processes, and few are saying that the pandemic has had a negative impact regarding the member's attachment to the society and to each other. It could be a matter of further study whether this is in correlation with the efforts put into institutional work, in meetings and shared reflections.

In these circumstances, each society searched for its own way of coping with newly imposed tasks, and they differed in this regard. There are variations regarding the time necessary to re-establish clinical praxis and training of candidates (some societies stopped this completely and only after a period of time, from several weeks to a year, continued working in a new, online manner, while some moved immediately to it); then with regard to the extent to which online clinical work was accepted and how long it went on during this period; and finally, concerning the general orientation towards online work after and beyond the time of the pandemic. For some societies and members, online clinical work, including training analyses, was completely unacceptable, and for most of them, this was accepted only for the period of urgency. The societies seem more willing to accept online meetings and scientific seminars, and rare are those which postponed all their activities, using the digital platform only for the general assembly.

A serious common concern is the impact of the pandemic on training. Several societies report that converting to a digital format (even supporting and maintaining a feeling of continuity in training and in relation to the society) affected the group of candidates, changing group coherence and group dynamics. Also, some responses mention a significant number of interruptions in training, and others an increasing number of applications for training during this period.

Some societies lost members, and this enlarged the burden of mourning. For some of them, the pandemic brought to the fore certain facts that they were not aware of – that 50 per cent of training analysts were over 70 years old and directly at risk because of age.

Many societies were engaged in public voluntary work.

War in Ukraine

This question is delicate for analysis, not only because of the real threatening danger and worries about the future, but also due to its duration, which renders the internal work unfinished and the responses incomplete. In the responses, most of which arrived in the period from July 2022 to January 2023, a general feeling of shock and anxiety prevailed, insecurity and fear for colleagues, both in Ukraine and in Russia. Three societies are under the direct impact of the war in different ways, depending on the sides of their countries.

On one side, many members and candidates have been forced to move to different countries. Training has been restored after many months, with the help of the Sponsoring Committee and the financial help of EPF/IPA, and is taking place only online. Questions of survival and safety came to the fore, as well as of providing members and candidates with the necessary help, of sustaining the training and the society as a whole. The activity and the engagement of the society's board are immense.

On the other side of the war, in a different way, there are efforts to survive and keep the society and training functioning, with many emigrating members and training analysts. Papers about war, totalitarianism, and propaganda are read and discussed; the paper "Psychoanalysis in Dark Times" about the history of psychoanalysis in Germany, Argentina, and Brazil in periods of dictatorship and totalitarianism was presented. The conference "Values" is planned, and many meetings on "how we can help each other" are being organised.

To some extent, the responses of other societies are influenced by their geographical and emotional closeness to the war zone, with immense fear and insecurity in the societies of countries close to the Ukrainian–Russian area. For some societies, the revival of their own traumatic past is also apparent.

This has brought the membership together, and it is another occasion, after the Covid-19 crises, in which the advantages of the organisations showed their potential, which is now broadly recognised: "if we had to say what has changed, it would be the awareness of the members and the consideration of the importance of an international community". There are many responses about the important role of the EPF and the IPA in this period (from donations and coordination of collected funds to organisations of exchanges, discussions and info boards, all the way to contributions to a general feeling of not being alone in the face of catastrophe, to feel cared for and helped).

Other crises are mentioned with a variety of responses: worries about the Iran crisis; the major economic crisis from 2012 to 2016; long and hard dictatorship in some countries; sudden, unexpected death of analysts with considerable power and status; attacks on psychoanalysis at universities, in psychiatric hospitals, in the health system; the killing of George Floyd; repeated exposure to crises triggered by the changes in the psychotherapeutic healthcare system; subordination of psychotherapy to legal constructions and to financial arbitrariness from health insurance providers; chronic acute trauma of the nineties; the fall of the Iron Curtain; environmental crisis; migrations of Latin American colleagues towards the end of the seventies and during the eighties; their creation of private and autonomous institutions that have operated in parallel with the society; the Russian invasion of Georgia in 2008; and the crisis of the Russian invasion of Crimea in 2014.

In conclusion, these are the main findings from the IMF survey. The nature of the survey just enables the mapping of potential points for further investigation. Only subsequent, thoughtful analysis, compared with other sources of data, like extensive unstructured IMF interviews which have been done with representatives of the various IPA societies in previous years, supported by written histories of the societies, will allow deeper conclusions and greater insight into the unconscious dynamics.

Note

1 The entire IMF group was engaged in collecting and data processing. The related text "Psychoanalytic organisations caught in the crossfire" was presented by Jasminka Šuljagić at the IPA congress in Cartagena in 2023, and "Input from the questionnaires" by Gabor Szonyi at the EPF Conference in Cannes 2023.

Part IX

Rebirth of Psychoanalytic Organisations

Ideal and Reality Then and Now

Chapter 20

A Split and a Merger

Experiencing the Dynamics of Reorganisation

Franziska Ylander

This is a story about the splitting of one society into two and about the work 40 years later to merge the two societies into one. The split created two societies, both – with time – turning into well-established organisations, coexisting in the same social and cultural context, but each with old wounds to heal.

I will tell the story focusing on organisation and work groups. Psychoanalytical thinking and interpretation are indispensable for understanding how things come about, *how it happened*. When you start looking into *how to achieve changes*, a group-oriented and less individualistic approach is more pragmatic, even indispensable, to enlighten the difficulties that will arise in the societies during the process.

Background

The Swedish Psychoanalytic Society was founded in the thirties and, during the decades to follow, kept up a classical Freudian profile. In the mid-sixties, there was a major crisis around a training analyst who was dismissed as such and who then chose to leave the society. The training analyst had a theoretical position different from that of the society and its institute, but the dismissal also had to do with other, rather-sensitive matters. The training analyst had a tight group of close followers who followed and who, all in solidarity with the dismissed training analyst, left as well, and a new society was created. Theoretically, this group had an interest in early, pre-Oedipal disturbances and in object relations theory and, accordingly, successfully developed an ambitious training programme.

After a decade, the same training analyst – the founding one – was dismissed from the "new" society, due to similar problems as had happened in the "old" one. Miraculously, and admirably, the "new" society (let me call it the "Association") survived this trauma. The "old" society (the "Society") prospered as well, and both had good training programmes, with not too different structures. During the decades to come, psychoanalysis was "en vogue", and both institutes had many candidates. Coexistence was possible.

Years went by, and little by little, the clinical and theoretical positions of the societies changed. The Society developed interests in object relations and in Bion's writings, much encouraged by the founding of a prosperous child analysis training.

DOI: 10.4324/9781032709819-30

The Association rediscovered the necessity of having a basic and thorough knowledge in Freud, combined and in tune with their deep interest in early disturbances. Teachers were exchanged for theoretical seminars at the training institutes. Rumours told that there were colleagues on the couches of the "other" society. Friendships were many; marriages happened. Combined peer groups for supervision and discussion, based on personal likings, also appeared. The child analysis training of the Society accepted members and candidates from the Association.

In the early nineties, 30 years after the "split", the first discussion about a possible rapprochement came up. Although there was general agreement that there would probably be a lot to gain from cooperation, not much happened on this issue at that moment. Instead, the Association, probably wisely, chose to go through the long process of becoming an IPA study group and, in 2005, was accepted as component society. Within the Association, this act of establishing an important aspect of identity was wisely given priority, and with very good reason, looking backwards.

Still, also other processes in the external world were of joint interest for both societies: There was (and still is) an aging population of active analysts. Both societies had a waning inflow of candidates, not to speak of analysands. Both societies put huge resources into very ambitious training institutes. There were first informal, and then also formal, discussions between the two boards and institutes. In 2007, a "decision of intention" was taken by both boards, implying that the societies jointly should investigate and analyse the preconditions for a fusion – or as it finally turned out – a merging.

The Work Group for a Possible Merging

A group was created – four senior analysts, two from each society, were asked to perform the task of investigating the possibilities for the getting together of the two societies. The two boards formulated a very clear commission which was, I think, instrumental in making it possible for the group to work very efficiently during the rather short time allotted. It is of utmost importance to underline the necessity for and impact of this very clear formulation of the task as a condition for a successful endeavour for a work group like ours – I was one of the members.

The work group started its work in September 2007 and delivered its final report after 18 months. The report concluded in a strong recommendation to go through with a merging of the societies. The boards then took over, and from March 2009, when the proposal to merge was presented to the membership, different formal steps were taken in both societies up to the final merging in May 2010.

There is, of course, a lot to be said about how the work group went about its work, but let me just state that besides mapping and comparing the different parts and aspects of the two societies by extensive interviews, questionnaires, and meetings, we tried to achieve as much transparency as possible towards both societies, publishing newsletters to the memberships about the proceeding work every third month, arranging three open meetings for all members for open discussions – the first one on "the past", the second on "today", and lastly "future". We also kept in mind the fact that however much you try to inform, there will always be members who angrily argue that they never have been told.

Among many things, the WG suggested a period of observance on how the societies were represented in the new board, institute, committees, etc. This is particularly interesting looking back, regarding the conscious intentions to escape rivalry in the name of justice. As it turned out, we were probably thereby – unconsciously and defensively – also trying to avoid feelings of loss and pain.

Merger Group – The Follow-Up

In November 2011, one year and a half after the inauguration of the Swedish Psychoanalytic Association (SPA), a follow-up study was initiated by the board by appointing a "fusion group", later named "merger group" (MG), also consisting of four other senior members from the "old societies". Focus was on finding out to what extent the different groups – board of society, board of institute, different committees for admission, outreach, etc. – had clearly formulated *aims for their work*, and to what extent the members could see their work as *part of a larger context*, primarily the new Swedish Psychoanalytic Association (Berge et al., 2018).

In the interviews, it was obvious that the idea of one's own society being extinguished, annihilated, liquidated – you name it – had been repelling. This notwithstanding, most members were quite satisfied with the process so far, and people were not particularly interested in whoever had his/her origin in "the other society". Also, what was rather striking, differences in opinion were usually not along lines of difference of "origin". Perhaps the concept of "*merging*" was ingenious, and rather easily accepted. It is, of course, interesting to speculate to what extent this is/was defensive in keeping painful matters undercover, and in that case, if this defensive reaction was "for better or for worse".

The notion of "homelessness" came up in several ways. Homelessness was, on a manifest level, obvious, considering that one of the two societies gave up their offices and had to squeeze into the slightly larger offices of the old society. But it also appeared that feelings of sadness and loss had something to do with reappearing difficulties in finding one's identity as a psychoanalyst, probably triggered and highlighted by the turmoil released by the merging. As already pointed out, the reality of a diminishing number of full-time analysts had been of primary importance in initiating the first steps towards the joint "letter of intention" already in 2007. But this problem area was not consciously or clearly very well acknowledged within the new Association, at least not during the first two years of observation. In the follow-up study, this negligence was observed and understood as part of and contributing to the mourning process, expressed by several members as a rather specific fantasy. Many members seemed to imagine the existence of a place where the "true analysts" are. This idealised place is inhabited by analysts in full-time practice, and from this place – paradise – one is expelled or not allowed.

Most members earn most of their living working as psychotherapists and/or in psychiatry, similar in both societies. The fantasy appeared to be independent of the merging itself but triggered by a concrete change of home/office lodgings and not consciously perceived feelings of inevitable change and loss.

Structural Themes: Two Years After Merging and Up to 2018

In their analysis of the interview material, the merger group focused on structural themes. It was clearly stated that it usually takes more than five years before a new culture and new working models following a fusion can find its shape and form. In the board and the institute, the elected chairs of participating committees sometimes had difficulties in integrating their personal position with a common, not quite clearly defined task. This unclarity can probably be understood as anticipations of imagined or real differences brought up when fusion had turned into reality.

This obviously seemed to lead to what the merger group called "a too democratic" way of letting everyone have his/her say, and as counterpart, a heightened consciousness, perhaps even suspiciousness, among the members of the group about hidden power structures, power balance, and so on. Groups with clearly defined and concrete tasks managed to work in a more smooth and uncomplicated way. For instance, after an initial crisis around a particular case, the committee for admission of candidates managed to formulate clearly stated rules concerning basic formal qualifications for becoming a candidate, supported and then decided by the board of the Association. Thereby it became possible for the group to work on the task of interviewing and to concentrate on the delicate judgements of suitability, the preconditions and the relation to the institute having been clarified.

At the other end of the spectrum, we find the training and the candidates. Both societies were working in the Eitingon model. The work to change and/or combine differences in focus, to allocate teaching resources, to give and take in everything concerning content and planning of the theoretical seminars – all this put huge demands on the committee for theoretical seminars, as well as and on the teachers. Looking back at the first years of fusion of the trainings, how John Steiner describes the mourning process as loss of the object and the experience of loss comes to mind as extremely meaningful concepts. In hindsight, candidates obviously felt rather at the mercy of things they could not control, and likewise, the seminar committee did not feel supported by the institute, which struggled with unexpected uncertainties, and unclarity about its new position.

A similar situation appeared in the committee for clinical supervision. This group – as all committees composed by members from both societies – had, on a conscious level, a conviction of unity and shared ideas. This turned out differently in reality, and hard work had to be done not to turn this into a problem for the candidates in ongoing clinical supervisions.

The merger group underscored the role of impact and the importance of *the chair* of every working committee. One must be extraordinarily careful and caring in stating clearly what is the mandate of the chair, and thereby his/her group, in relation to the formally higher level, regardless of whether it is institute or board of society. This might concern deciding how to interpret the rules of a training model or of who is duly formally qualified to be accepted as a candidate, teacher, or training analyst. In the end, when unclarity takes over at the higher levels, it is always striking back at the ones at the lowest level, that is, the candidates.

I am sure that this is not just happening in societies in transition – it is part of the lifetime of all kinds of organisations. But the situation I have been talking about – a merging of two societies – certainly gives us an exceptional and useful possibility to highlight problems we would otherwise not have observed.

Reference

Berge, A., Boalt Boethius, S., Flygare, K., & Hamreby, M. (2018). *Merger and now what?* Report from the Swedish Psychoanalytic Association.

Chapter 21

Rebirth of Psychoanalytic Organisations

Ideal and Reality Then and Now – Exemplified in the Hungarian Psychoanalytical Society

Gábor Szőnyi

Taking the Hungarian society as an example, I show the vicissitudes of idealisation–des-idealisation in the life of analytic organisations.

We can explore organisational idealisation from three viewpoints: idealisation–des-idealisation of key figures; idealisation–des-idealisation of the analytic group/society; and idealisation–des-idealisation of international psychoanalysis and of the international psychoanalytic organisations. Historically, idealisation–des-idealisation changes periodically. However, the three dimensions mentioned do not move together.

The Hungarian Psychoanalytical Society, founded in 1913, was among the first ones. At the very beginning, and retrospectively, Ferenczi was a key figure, both locally and internationally. As a key person, he was heroised, de-heroised, and re-heroised both internationally and locally – wiped out from the psychoanalytic community's intellectual exchange for decades. His diary, originally written in German, was introduced and was translated into Hungarian only in the seventies(!).

Due to world wars, economic crisis, and political earthquakes, many Hungarian analysts migrated in waves; many of those who remained were annihilated. Still, quite a bunch of analysts remained and gave full of hope, blossoming continuation of the organisation after WWII. The deep blow came in 1948–1949, when, under the pressure of the forming Soviet regime, the society "voluntarily" declared dissolution. No civil, NGO organisations were tolerated, except those under the communist party/government umbrella. During the next 30 years, the members of the original society could remain only secretly, just individually – *no more as a constituent society* – direct members of IPA. Privately, some of them continued to offer training analysis, and later seminars. Psychoanalysis, as such, was officially named as "the maiden servant of the bourgeoise", although psychanalysts were personally not persecuted.

The key figures of that time followed divergent routes, and in that respect, the Hungarian group fell apart. Looking back from the future, three to four key figures emerged, around whom small groupings formed. Each of those key figures was seen later as a hero, what a generation later determined, to a certain degree, the birth and internal-external conflicts of the new Hungarian Psychoanalytical Society.

DOI: 10.4324/9781032709819-31

One of the basic divergences was the relatedness and self-definition towards IPA. A few saw themselves as members of IPA and hold as much contact internationally as possible. For example, Imre Hermann thought his main mission was to maintain Hungarian psychoanalysis as part of IPA. Székács-Schönberger set up his own "one-person" psychoanalytic school, without searching for international integration. Another line – more comforting than the political regime – had not in mind to have anything to do with IPA but run their own psychotherapy trainings with psychoanalytical orientation.

In the late sixties, negotiations started with IPA about reestablishing Hungarian analysis by becoming again a component society, with hopes and suspicion from both sides. The IPA executive's provisions were that you cannot have a democratic organisation in a totalitarian regime. The key members from the original society felt a hostile attitude that IPA wanted to accept them on premises: site visit ("We should let us be assessed by those who were in napkins when we already had been analysts?") and study group status first.

The problem was solved by the constructive collaboration of the then formed IPA East European committee with active European members – and the new generation of analysts, trained by the Hungarian "oldies". They became the new/founding hero, mentioned until now as "The Fives" – without names, but everybody knows who they were.[1] Notwithstanding, the fact was that just one person (Hidas) took the personal risk to work and co-operate actively with IPA on re-establishing the Hungarian organisation. The controversies among the previous key persons – partly hidden, partly openly – repeated among the FIVES and, to some degree, are present also today.

The organisational solution was a kind of "gentlemen's agreement": The IPA did not publish in the roster that there was a Hungarian study group, but only the individual names in the "direct members'" part, to defend the Hungarian analysts from the authorities, because "forming an illegal organisation". In the document of agreement (signed by Widlöcher and Hidas), it was called "the unofficial Hungarian study group". On the other side, the analysts were allowed to form a "subsection psychoanalysis" *inside* the Hungarian Psychiatric Association, where only IPA members and candidates could participate. (Although, according to the by-laws, each member of the psychiatric association was free to join any of the sections/subsections.) This secured that there was a – legally not autonomous – practically autonomous local IPA analytic organisation.

From 1975 on, we had to go through all steps – site visit, study group, provisional society – until we became a new IPA component society in 1989. We got – especially because having been the only IPA inside analytic group from the Soviet imperium – extreme amount of help, both individually and as a group. In my view, both – the hostile-felt demand to be "just a **new** group as any other", and the helper–helped relationship syndrome – contributed to the idealisation–des-idealisation of the international organisations IPA and EPF, of the new Hungarian Psychoanalytical Society and ourselves as individual analysts.

The new Hungarian Psychoanalytical Society was officially and legally founded and became component IPA society in 1989, just together with the change of the political system. However, it had to give up the exceptional position, had to stand upon their own feet and to start the life of a small, weak, and unexperienced organisation. Anything else than something for idealisation.

In 1987, just before the IPA approval of our society as a component society, we made a simple, small survey among Hungarian analysts and candidates with the question: How do you see the general level of Hungarian analysts compared with "an average international analyst" in the different historical periods? The periods we created were the following: the 1910s; between WWI and WWII; during WWII; 1945–1948 (the short democratic revival in Hungary); 1949–1960 (hard dictatorship); 1961–1975 (lighter dictatorship); 1975– (study group status). The most important result was that until WWII, we ranked Hungarian analysts higher than "an average" international analyst. During WWII and the short democracy after, the respondents assessed Hungarian analysts being around the same level as "the average international analysts" are. But for the period immediately after the "voluntary" dissolution, actually, the same analysts' quality was ranked expressively lower compared with the international average. This trend of self-degradation got stronger for both next periods of hard and looser dictatorship and continued also during the process of organisational re-joining to the IPA: the Hungarian analysts – members of the new society – were seen by themselves and by their trainees being on much lower level than the international average. Another controversial result of the survey said that majority of the membership and candidates assessed the Hungarian analysts – without international comparison – good and competent, while the society as such hostile and ineffective (Szőnyi, 1988).

Unfortunately, we did not ask the respondents about their impression on the international organisations IPA and EPF. It was a period when many of us got personally international help to participate on conferences and at different other programs and had, through that, a lot of impressions.

The results challenge for interpretation. In my view, they exemplify the interplay between self-respect and self-confidence of the individuals as analysts, the inner respect and evaluation of the group/organisation to which they belong and the distance from – integration level into the larger professional community/organisation (e.g. IPA, EPF). Further, how broader external social-political factors can overshadow professional being.

Giving a glimpse to the different objects and dimensions of idealisation, in a study on the training experiences obtained in the EPI, we found that idealisation goes a typical arc (Szőnyi et al., 2017):

- When I will become a psychoanalyst, I will be one of the chosen ones (idealisation of the group of analysts).
- Goes over, while in training analysis, onto the personal analyst.
- Which goes over, after having finished personal analysis but being still in supervision with the first cases, onto the supervisor.
- Which might go over, when the candidate becomes an "equal" with the previous training analyst and supervisor, onto psychoanalysis and psychoanalytic organisations as such.

Of course, there is always a to-and-back between idealisation and des-idealisation. Because of the strong tendency for idealisation, des-idealisation takes stronger part at all mentioned steps/aspects/dimensions too.

In the shadow of the – maybe over-idealised – great ancestors, instead of increase, we experienced decrease of self-respect of Hungarian colleagues as analysts. A possible consequence was that, while in our theoretical training they were mentioned, we did not try to integrate their works into the flow of the international theoreticians and the general development of psychoanalytic theory/technique. I would say that the famous Hungarian analysts, the representatives of the Budapest school of psychoanalysis, remain museum figures, while the reference persons to be idealised were the outstanding "Western", "international" ones. This disregard is clearly mirrored in the publication references of the new generation Hungarian analysts in the Hungarian psychoanalytic journal *Lélekelemzés* (*Psychoanalysis*). The "downgrading" strengthened the splits between "analytic veterans" and the new generations and also contributed to the continuous ambivalent-negative feelings toward the international psychoanalytic organisations. (A responsible component could be that you extremely rarely idealise your peers or members of the closer generation.)

From our society forum's discussions and the experiences of the European Psychoanalytic Institute comes the following:

A special route of key figures idealisation we frequently meet in the history of those EE new psychoanalytic organisations, where there was no own tradition of psychoanalysis. 1–3 analysts, who returned to their country after the fall of the Soviet Union, presented/represented the psychoanalysis of those countries where they had been trained, somehow as the representant of those key figures of international psychoanalysis from whom they had learned, by whom they had been trained. This in-person transfer resulted in similar "original split formation", we inherited in Hungary from our three (or FIVES).

Original unsolved conflicts and crises are seen as usually negative because they threaten with annihilation of the organisation. Therefore, there is robust tendency to masque and deny those developmental events. Signs and tools of warding off are, for example:

• Over-idealisation of the own group (and psychoanalysis) as opposed to the surrounding local other psychotherapeutic organisations
• Turning inward and fortification of "internal solidarity"
• Over-idealisation of the first generation and seeing them as irreplaceable (among others, by keeping them in offices for several turns)
• Avoidance of controversies in scientific discussions

In the first decades of the new Hungarian group/society, we can observe all those mentioned.

From the new, young psychoanalytic organisations' point of view, we might assume that the almost-splits at the beginnings have the function of bringing to the surface forces which have, simultaneously, cohesive *and* disruptive character. If there is a capacity to face those events as challenges and the group invests into creative discussions, the society survives and develops instead of stagnation or early disintegration.

My personal observation – which misses research underpinning – is that those evolving analytic/psychotherapeutic organisations which start with and remain in an (over-idealised) one-person-founded, cone-shaped system do not survive the third change of the leadership generations.

Of course, idealisations will be counterbalanced by des-idealisation. Des-idealisation of the own group, because it is weak and small among, and compared with, the other IPA component organisations. Opposite to this, the analytic group is seen with envy and respect in the local professional psychotherapy field, which strengthens the feeling of superiority.

On the individuals' level, I feel myself professionally weak and insignificant in the international community of analysts, which might contribute to the des-idealisation of the international psychoanalytic organisations. Emotionally, and in contacts, most of us distance from the international organisations, which are seen far away, bureaucratic, and demanding.

A small example for the controversial dynamics: In the first years of the autonomous Hungarian society, advanced candidates demanded that the training committee approve the analyses which they provide to trainees of other psychotherapy methods as official training therapy. When it was refused, they founded a separate society for psychoanalytically oriented psychotherapy, where they were immediately accepted as training therapists.

And what is the playground of reality? I think, the need for idealisation and des-idealisation is an essential part of the training for and the practising of psychoanalysis. It helps to maintain our commitment for and capacity to a type of working, which we then describe as relaxed as an impossible profession.

Note

1 György Hidas, Adorján Linczényi, Lívia Nemes, György Vikár, Teréz Virág.

References

Szőnyi, G. (1988). About some problematical aspects of psychoanalytical identity in Hungary. Paper read at the *Symposium on psychoanalysis. A Hungarian – American dialogue*. Manuscript.

Szőnyi, G., Kardos, T., Stromme, H., & Vassilev, S. (2017). From motivation to organizational integration: Training experiences of recently qualified psychoanalysts. In K. Martin & M. Siegward (Eds.), *Psychology research progress. Psychoanalytic theory: A review and directions for research* (pp. 1–64). Nova Science Publishers.

Chapter 22

Rebirth of Psychoanalytic Organisations

Ideal and Reality Then and Now, Using the Example of the Vienna Psychoanalytic Society

Christine Diercks

The birth of the Vienna Psychoanalytic Society, with Freud at its centre, served as a model for the birth of the other local psychoanalytic institutions who, together, founded the IPA in 1910. This is part of our common history and – idealised – our myth of origin.

1938–1945

Reflecting on the rebirth of the Vienna Psychoanalytic Society in 1946, the desired ideal then was closely linked to loss: the complete loss of the society and its institutions, the loss of its members, and the loss of Sigmund Freud, caused by the NS regime, which took over power in Austria in 1938. Freud and almost all – mostly Jewish – members were under pressure to leave the country to save their lives. Not all succeeded. The NS attack was directed at the core components of psychoanalysis, its institutions and their Jewish members, while the therapeutic potential of psychoanalysis – purified of Freud's libido theory and the Jews – was to be put at the service of the murderous regime. By the end of 1938, three members of the WPV were still living in Vienna: Alfred Winterstein, who survived the Nazi period in great seclusion; Richard Nepalek, who is only known to have died in Vienna of "gas poisoning" (1940); and also August Aichhorn, who remained in Vienna and tried to rebuild a new psychoanalytic group, first secretly and, from 1941 on, within the so-called "Göring Institut" in Berlin, where they were recognised as a training group. This group consisted not only of potential psychoanalysts but also of Adlerians; additionally, some members close to the NS regime took part in the training.

The period 1938–1945 has been studied in a research project, and the results are available in the form of three books[1]. About the period after 1945, however, we know much less, and we will try to continue the research concrete preliminary work has already begun.

1945–1971

After the war, the group split up immediately, and its psychoanalytic part became the core of the re-established Vienna Psychoanalytic Society. This was informally

DOI: 10.4324/9781032709819-32

approved by Ernest Jones, the president of the IPA, already in 1946, and officially at the IPA Congress in Zurich in 1949, thanks to Jones and the close relationship between Aichhorn and Anna Freud.

After the war, psychoanalysis in Vienna had to regain foothold in a country full of severely traumatised people, where now victims, survivors of the resistance, NS perpetrators, followers, and bystanders had to live together in a destroyed world, full of pain, shame, and guilt, which too often was denied. Nothing was as it had been before the war, neither in the city nor in the small cosmos of the re-founded Vienna Psychoanalytic Society. The thread of continuity was extremely fragile. Only two members – Aichhorn and Winterstein – of the old society still lived in Vienna in 1945, for a short time supported by Otto Fleischmann, Walter Hollitscher, and Hans Jokl. Nevertheless, Aichhorn presented an ambitious and comprehensive organisation chart for the society, its training institute, outreach activities, counselling, and the free clinic. This small group wanted to rebuild the former society but suffered from a lack of resources of all kinds, especially that of experienced training analysts.

In spite of all efforts, the group almost collapsed after Aichhorn's death in 1949, when Winterstein became president. Deeply devoted to Sigmund Freud, the few post-war analysts tried to re-anchor and preserve his teaching – holding on to Freudian drive theory in the face of other schools of psychoanalysis, which was most important to stabilise the fragile psychoanalytic identity. The society's public face was, for a long time, one of authority, of orthodoxy, but also of reservation, rigidity, and inhibition. All efforts in this small group were concentrated on the training of a new generation of psychoanalysts and on a way to save the lost.

When Wilhelm Solms became president in 1957 after Winterstein, he said of his program, "[E]ducation is our main task. After 1945, the Society resisted the temptation to noisily draw attention to psychoanalysis. We have the task of being a place of serious training" (Huber, 1977, p. 89).

1971 First Achievements

In 1971, psychoanalysts made a vital contribution to establish the Freud Museum in Berggasse 19. In the same year, the International Psychoanalytical Congress was held in Vienna; it was on this occasion that Anna Freud made her first return to Vienna since her escape. Also, the "Tiefenpsychologische Institut" (Depth Psychology Institute), today the Clinic for Psychoanalysis and Psychotherapy, was established at the medical faculty of Vienna University. An additional training in child analysis in the Anna Freud tradition was offered within the training institute of the Vienna Psychoanalytic Society.

Wilhelm Solms – urgently looking for international exchange and help – played a major role in setting up the Middle European Seminars, the later German-speaking psychoanalytic conferences. He was also engaged in the foundation of the European Psychoanalytical Federation (1966–1969) as a forum for mutual scientific exchange and therefore became its second president.

Controversies and Development

Freud became an important figure for the student movement: bright and dedicated young minds found their way to psychoanalysis in the post-1968 years. They not only dealt critically with the post-war society and the idea of Austria as the first victim of the Nazis but also dared to question psychoanalytic positions.

I became a candidate in the WPV in the 1980s – after the period of ensuring the survival of psychoanalysis in Vienna had ended. We were not obliged to uphold Freud so rigorously anymore, with the number of members and training analysts increasing and the conditions for training becoming better. Finally, it was possible for us to take the risk to discuss and adopt post-Freudian developments too.

It always is a risk, because the moment of introducing something new, opening a new perspective, has not only a creative but also a violent, aggressive quality – attacking the common thinking, questioning those to whom we owe everything. This is a common situation in any development, as we know. The ability to face this depends on individual and collective circumstances, and in this country, actual persecution und real mass murder had taken place not so long ago.

The beginning of the debate about the Kleinian approach in the late 1980s/early 1990s was accompanied by quite violent discussions. The leading idea of our society until then – one can say our ideal – had been to uphold Freud's drive theory and retrieve what had been lost. The horrible risk in that controversy was to face the underlying meanings and fantasies, to attack Freud again, to persecute the Jewish Freudians, to destroy psychoanalysis once more.[2]

1991–1999: Reopening the Psychoanalytic Free Clinic – the Ambulatorium

At the same time, a similar process on an institutional level took place. A group of candidates started a project for reopening the psychoanalytic free clinic. Though everybody wanted this, it was difficult for the established members to accept, to tolerate these active candidates. It was a highly ambivalent situation for everyone, which we finally tried to structure by introducing procedural rules.

But again, the act of fighting for the project confronted us with history and the fear of doing something in the sense of being a "Täter" (a "doer"/perpetrator), always in the light of the monstrosities which had taken place. Being aware of this might have been also an attempt of unfreezing, of release.

Somewhat pointedly formulated, most of us today are children and grandchildren of the victims and the perpetrators. It is no longer about our lives, about our own crime. But our capacity to work together is in danger, our creativity, our free thinking, our individual integrity, and our ability to contain such feelings and fantasies, such confrontations with explicit or unspoken aspects of monstrous quality. It took me a long time to face and to accept that as part of my and of our heritage.

"Being Jewish in a fantasized or real hostile environment", as a member recently put it in memoriam of a colleague, referred not only to the social situation in Austria but also to the small cosmos within our psychoanalytic society (WPV). For her, "the most important conflict in the WPV was the one about the Nazi era in the 1980s and how it had affected the WPV after 1945. The struggle to restore child analysis and its importance in Vienna was almost part of it". The dynamics of the disputes sometimes overwhelmed and paralyzed us. We tried to discuss these within our society, but our capacity was limited, most discussions taking place in smaller groups or privately. Many of us were interested in history; we built up an archive, we published, we did research.

Part of us became specially committed to developing our institutions and took the risk to decide and act, to be responsible, to make mistakes, to succeed and to fail – not only in this monstrous dimension, but also as part of usual matters, average life. When we, for instance, reopened the free clinic, there was a lot to do on a pragmatic level: a period of public affairs started, because introducing and running the clinic required public relations on various levels, with social institutions as well as with politicians. We also had to develop business models, deal with financial matters, communication, and team building. And above all, we had to develop psychoanalytically. A whole group of candidates tried hard and was very devoted – to the free clinic and to psychoanalysis. Supported by the whole society, 61 years after its liquidation, our Ambulatorium could open its doors again. It was a touching moment for all of us. And we had learned a lot – on many levels – and this prepared us for facing the coming challenges and crises.

2005: Crises, Further Steps, Reorganisation

Although the Vienna Psychoanalytic Society was basically still on a good way and had a lot of potential, a few years later, in 2004, we faced a serious crisis because of a profound lack of public relations (at that time, we had severe conflicts with the board of the Sigmund Freud Society, which, before, had been something like our "foreign office"). In addition, we had to face the change of the legal situation for our training and of the insurance's reimbursement of sessions, an increasingly difficult situation for high-frequency psychoanalysis in the psychosocial field. A "psychoanalysis light" business idea, successfully performed by a so-called "Sigmund Freud University", became very dominant. One could say we were confronted with the limits of our volunteer work, a meanwhile insufficient organisation model, and with a lack of public relations.

Supported by the fact that the other local psychoanalytic group, the Vienna Psychoanalytic Association, applied for IPA membership and provoked by severe crises in both groups, in 2005, a close collaboration between the Vienna Psychoanalytic Society and the Vienna Psychoanalytic Association (WAP) began. This started with the joint holding of the Sigmund Freud Lectures, a series of conferences that is still successful today.

In 2006, this collaboration finally led to the founding of a joint "Wiener Psychoanalytische Akademie" (Vienna Psychoanalytic Academy, owned 50:50 by the Vienna Psychoanalytic Association and the Society), a centre for psychoanalysis and its applications that is also accessible to the public. It provides an institutional framework for training, transmission, and research work, interdisciplinary exchange, and project-based collaboration. Interdisciplinary-oriented, the academy builds a bridge between those who practice classical psychoanalysis and those who are clinically or theoretically interested in psychoanalysis without immediately seeking a full psychoanalytic training.

In 2007, the two psychoanalytic groups moved into new premises together. We rented a whole floor, the rooms of the two groups separated by a firewall and connected by doors and by the joint academy. At the beginning, we did not dare to dream how successful the academy would be. Our house is full today, usually seven days a week. To tell this story would fill a separate paper.

I would just like to mention that it was very important that we started not only inviting internationally recognised authorities to lecture in Vienna but also increasingly took over the lectures ourselves. We particularly encouraged young colleagues to present what they are working on, what they are thinking about, to discuss it with others; we also involved them in teaching on an early stage of their career.

Training Under Ideal/Optimal/Realistic Conditions, IPA Standards, EPF, EVP

In Vienna, the psychoanalytic training follows the Eitingon model based on a four- to five-times-a-week setting. Part of the training is organised in cooperation between WPV and WAP. Embedded in a postgraduate master's program, it has recently even become possible to complete the training in cooperation with the Department of Psychoanalysis and Psychotherapy at the Medical University. The cooperation with this department has a long tradition and bridges the gap between our psychoanalytic institutions and the Medical University.

Till today, we are a member of the IPA, and following the IPA Eitingon model always had a deep meaning for us. It was not only a benchmark and support in turbulent times. We do not protect the high-frequency setting in training as a fetish, a compulsive ritual, or an elitist idea, but it helps to support the candidates to experience a model of best standards conditions for psychoanalysis – their own and the analyses of their patients. Once they are on solid ground here, as soon as they are identified in a good sense, they can modify their setting without everything becoming arbitrary.

But looking at the history of these international IPA training standards rules, the situation was always complex, and still is. Therefore, a few years ago, the IPA unexpectedly gave in to pressure, particularly strong from Latin America, to lower the educational standards of the Eitingon model. This caused great concern not only in our society but also with other European groups. Now, the previous backing by the IPA is gone, and we are in a paradox situation: we maintain standards that even the IPA has abandoned. Of course, the IPA does not forbid us to do so, but it has undermined our position in the public debate about high-frequency psychoanalysis. And paradoxically enough, the other Viennese IPA group – the Vienna Psychoanalytic Association – which introduced the four-hour setting on its way to IPA membership, now is a member of an IPA that says that this is no longer required.

Also, the way in which this decision was taken by the IPA caused great irritation with many of us, not only in Vienna, but also in other European IPA societies too. They were confronted with a decision that was made over their heads. In response, the Vienna Society and the Association have joined the European Visiting Program (EVP), and they have started with exchange visits for European societies to reflect their training model from a clinical and scientific point of view, discussing the training experiences and learning from each other.

Psychoanalytic-Orientated Psychotherapy (POP)

But also in Vienna, there is a great need for low-frequency psychoanalytic psychotherapy, based on a two-times-a-week setting. There is a need for training and a need expressed by patients who cannot afford full analysis, or in the case that classical analysis is not indicated or not possible. We did not want to reduce the requirements for psychoanalytic training but introduced a separate training course in psychoanalytic-oriented psychotherapy (POP) in our academy. The introduction of this training was quite controversial among our members, but now it is firmly established. I think it is very important that this training take place in our house and not in a private setting or within other organisations. Both clinical methods can benefit from each other if they manage not to overly compete with each other but act complementary. There are also ways to change from one training into the other – both directions. Since the introduction of POP, the interest in psychoanalytic training has not decreased but even increased.

Traumatic and Unavoidable Crises, Conflicts and Developments, Current Challenges

The unique tradition of the Vienna Psychoanalytic Society, but also the experience of its destruction, has always constituted a great responsibility and challenge for most of its members to do their best to create good conditions for psychoanalysis in Vienna.

For us today, it is important to advance the scientific discussion without neglecting the interdisciplinary dimension. The psychoanalytic approach must be represented at the level of science and health policy, as well as in our public relations in general. Clinical training and further education in classical psychoanalysis and other therapeutic applications will always be a central task of psychoanalytic societies, and also due to legal regulations, a rapprochement with university institutions will take place.

These are complex tasks that require constant investment and renewal. Big new projects we often start with enthusiasm and devotion. "In love with beginning", J. B. Pontalis once headlined. You do everything for a baby or when you are in love.

But for intimate relations as well dynamics in institutions to survive, it is crucial that idealisation stops and limits are drawn, projects finally become business as usual, other interests come to the fore, the players change, and the generations change. That is the way things go, but it is not trivial – not for the young, not for the old – and although we are psychoanalysts, we underestimate the crises that we have to face in this context personally, but also in our institutions.

But the realisation of our projects also requires an appropriate infrastructure, and organisational and economic principles must be continuously developed. For those who are in charge, the principle of volunteering reaches its limits here. For the operation of our outpatient clinic and the academy, the economic conditions have already been improved step by step, so that today one can actually live from the work that is done there.

With all this in mind, one can be amazed that our society has been maintained for over a century, testifying to the undiminished potentiality of psychoanalysis.

Notes

1 See Aichhorn, 2012; Ash & Aichhorn, 2010; Ash, 2012.
2 Today we discuss all psychoanalytic schools and integrate new developments. In this orthodox sense, most of us are no longer Freudians, but many of us know Freud very well. Since 2012, an interdisciplinary team has also been working on a historical-critical Sigmund Freud edition, which is re-editing the work and the correspondence according to strictly scientific criteria.

References

Aichhorn, T. (Hg.). (2012). Die Psychoanalyse kann nur dort gedeihen, wo Freiheit des Gedankens herrscht: Briefwechsel 1921–1949. Anna Freud/August Aichhorn. In *Band 2 der Reihe Brüche und Kontinuitäten in der Geschichte der Wiener Psychoanalytischen Vereinigung 1938–1945*. Brandes & Apsel.
Ash, M. (Hg.). (2012). Materialien zur Geschichte der Psychoanalyse in Wien 1938–1945. In *Band 3 der Reihe Brüche und Kontinuitäten in der Geschichte der Wiener Psychoanalytischen Vereinigung 1938–1945*. Brandes & Apsel.
Ash, M., & Aichhorn, T. (Hg.). (2010). Psychoanalyse in totalitären und autoritären Regimen. In *Band 1 der Reihe Brüche und Kontinuitäten in der Geschichte der Wiener Psychoanalytischen Vereinigung 1938–1945*. Brandes & Apsel.
Huber, W. (1977). *Psychoanalyse in Österreich seit 1933*. Geyer.

Index

For Product Safety Concerns and Information please contact our EU
representative GPSR@taylorandfrancis.com
Taylor & Francis Verlag GmbH, Kaufingerstraße 24, 80331 München, Germany

www.ingramcontent.com/pod-product-compliance
Lightning Source LLC
Chambersburg PA
CBHW050656280326
41932CB00015B/2936